The International Court of Justice and Maritime Disputes

The origins of the maritime dispute between Chile and Peru go back to 1952, when these countries, along with Ecuador, asserted sovereignty over 200 nautical miles from their coasts. This maritime claim is widely regarded as one of the most important contributions by a group of developing countries to the law of the sea. Peru then asked the Court of International Justice to delimit its lateral boundary with Chile in accordance with principles of international law. Chile asked the Court to dismiss the request. The question before the ICJ Justice was whether the treaty concluded by the parties when they made their claim had also delimited their lateral boundary.

This book provides a critical analysis of the approach to treaty interpretation by the International Court of Justice in Maritime Disputes. Focusing on the case of Chile and Peru, the book explores two main issues: the interpretation of the Santiago Declaration and its connected treaties; and the tacit agreement that established a lateral maritime boundary with a seaward extension of 80 nautical miles. Part I argues that the Court's finding that the Santiago Declaration did not delimit the lateral boundary is mistaken because it ignores its context, as well as its object and purpose. Part II argues that the finding that the parties had entered into a tacit agreement is an unjustified legal inference derived from a hasty interpretation of the Special Agreement of 1954. It questions that the reliability of the evidence used to determine the seaward extent of the lateral boundary and argues that the Court failed to demonstrate the bearing of contemporaneous developments in the law of the sea on the content of the tacit agreement.

Julio Faundez is Professor of Law (Emeritus) at Warwick University, UK. He provided advice to the Chilean Foreign Ministry during this case.

Routledge Research in the Law of the Sea

Available titles in this series include:

The International Court of Justice and Maritime Disputes
The Case of Chile and Peru
Julio Faundez

The International Court of Justice and Maritime Disputes

The Case of Chile and Peru

Julio Faundez

Routledge
Taylor & Francis Group

LONDON AND NEW YORK

First published 2019
by Routledge

2 Park Square, Milton Park, Abingdon, Oxfordshire OX14 4RN
52 Vanderbilt Avenue, New York, NY 10017

Routledge is an imprint of the Taylor & Francis Group, an informa business

First issued in paperback 2020

British Library Cataloguing-in-Publication Data
A catalogue record for this book is available from the British Library

Library of Congress Cataloging-in-Publication Data
Names: Faundez, Julio, author.
Title: The International Court of Justice and maritime disputes: the case of Chile and Peru / Julio Faundez.
Description: Abingdon, Oxon; New York, NY: Routledge, 2018. | Includes bibliographical references and index.
Identifiers: LCCN 2018025597 | ISBN 9781138343320 (hbk)
Subjects: LCSH: Peru—Trials, litigation, etc. | Chile—Trials, litigation, etc. | Maritime boundaries—Peru. | Maritime boundaries—Chile. | Peru—Boundaries—Chile. | Chile—Boundaries—Peru. | Treaties—Interpretation and construction. | International Court of Justice.
Classification: LCC KZA1128.P47 F38 2018 | DDC 341.4/48091641—dc23
LC record available at https://lccn.loc.gov/2018025597

ISBN: 978-1-138-34332-0 (hbk)
ISBN: 978-0-367-60687-9 (pbk)

Typeset in Times New Roman
by codeMantra

To Anne, again

Contents

List of figures   xi
Abbreviations   xiii

Introduction   1

PART I
The Santiago Declaration and connected treaties   7
   A. Background 7
   B. Overview: approach to treaty interpretation 12
      1. Literal meaning 12
      2. Inadequate analysis of the Santiago Declaration 14
      3. Disregard of context 15
        (a) A note on context 16
        (b) The standard clause in the Lima Agreements 18
      4. Disregard of the practice of the parties 19
        (a) The Accession Protocol 20
        (b) Negotiations with Bolivia 21
   C. Object, purpose and context 22
      1. In general 22
      2. The Santiago Declaration 22
      3. The 1954 Lima Agreements 25
   D. Development of Paragraph IV 27
      1. Minutes of the Santiago Declaration 27
      2. Minutes of the Complementary Convention 32
      3. Minutes of the Agreement Relating to a Special
        Maritime Frontier Zone 34
      4. A note on the Minutes 36
   E. The 1968–1969 Lighthouse Arrangements 39
   F. Ordinary meaning and context 40
   G. Final remarks 43

PART II

The tacit agreement   45
  A. *Reasoning and evidence 45*
      1. Inference versus legal interpretation 45
      2. Agreement or evolving understanding? 49
  B. *Content of the Agreement 53*
      1. Nature of the boundary 53
      2. Extent of the lateral boundary 54
          (a) Practice of the parties: hunting and fishing 56
              i)   *Small vessels 57*
              ii) *Whale hunting 58*
              iii) *Fishing activities 60*
  C. *Contemporaneous law of the sea 63*
      1. Purpose of the inquiry 63
      2. State practice 64
      3. Role of the International Law Commission 65
          (a) Delimitation proposals 66
          (b) Breadth of the territorial sea 68
      4. Territorial sea and fisheries jurisdiction 70
          (a) An ambiguous statement 70
          (b) The six-plus-six formula 72
          (c) The 1958 Fisheries Convention 74
      5. The 200 mile claim 76
          (a) Validity and enforceability 76
          (b) Protests, acceptance and acquiescence 81
          (c) The claim endures 82
  D. *Final remarks 84*
      1. Evidence 84
      2. Equity 85

Conclusion   87

Annex 1: Declaration on the Maritime Zone (1952)   91
Annex 2: Complementary Convention to the
Declaration of Sovereignty over the Maritime Zone of
Two Hundred Miles (1954)   93
Annex 3: Agreement Relating to a Special Maritime
Frontier Zone (1954)   95
Annex 4: Agreements between Chile, Ecuador and
Peru concluded in 1952 and 1954   97

References   99
   Cases 99
   Official documents 99
   Minutes 100
   Books and articles in journals 100
Index   107

List of figures

I.1   Boundary lines claimed by Chile and Peru   2
I.2   Course of the maritime boundary   4

Abbreviations

CCM	Counter-Memorial of the Government of Chile
CEP countries	Chile, Ecuador and Peru
CORFO	State Development Corporation (Chile)
CR	Rejoinder of the Government of Chile
Compte Rendu	Verbatim Record, ICJ Hearings
EEZ	Exclusive Economic Zone
FAO	Food and Agriculture Organization
ICJ	International Court of Justice
ILC	International Law Commission
Minutes 1952 First Session	PM Annex 56
Minutes 1952 Second Session	CCM Annex 34
Minutes 1954 First Session	CCM Annex 38
Minutes 1954 Second Session	CCM Annex 39
nm	nautical miles
PCIJ	Permanent Court of International Justice
PM	Memorial of the Government of Peru
PR	Reply of the Government of Peru
UNCLOS	UN Convention on the Law of the Sea
VCLT	Vienna Convention on the Law of Treaties
YILC	Yearbook of the International Law Commission

References in the text

Direct quotations and references to the Judgment (I.C.J Reports 2014, 3) are identified in brackets by the number of the paragraph, e.g. (#56).

Direct quotations and references to the Opinions of Judges are identified in brackets by the number of the paragraph, preceded by the name of the Judge, e.g. (Owada #3).

Introduction

This study provides a critical analysis of the approach to treaty interpretation by the International Court of Justice in the *Maritime Dispute between Peru and Chile* (I.C.J Reports 2014, 3).

The origins of this dispute go back to 1952, when Chile, Peru and Ecuador made one of the most celebrated maritime claims of the twentieth century by asserting sovereignty over 200 nautical miles (nm) from their coasts. Their claim had a huge impact on the development of the law of the sea. It contributed to shaping the agenda of three successive Law of the Sea Conferences, leading ultimately to the universal recognition of the Exclusive Economic Zone, a 200 nm maritime zone under the jurisdiction and control of coastal states. The parties' claim is also significant since it was the first time that a group of developing countries managed successfully to challenge traditional international legal doctrine.

All cases decided by the Court merit close analysis. In this case, the Judgment is especially interesting because its findings were not anticipated, its reasoning was unconvincing and it completely disregarded the legal impact of the parties' 200 nm claim.

Peru asked the Court to delimit its lateral boundary with Chile in accordance with principles of international law. Chile, claiming that the parties had delimited their boundary in the *Santiago Declaration* of 1952, asked the Court to dismiss the request (see Figure I.1). The task of the Court should have been straightforward: first it had to decide whether the *Declaration* had delimited the parties' lateral boundary; and, secondly, in the event of a negative finding, it had to delimit the boundary.

The Court, however, did not follow this itinerary. It rejected Chile's claim, but found nonetheless that the parties had delimited their lateral boundary by means of a tacit agreement. This finding was prompted by a reference to the boundary in Article 1 of the 1954 *Special Maritime*

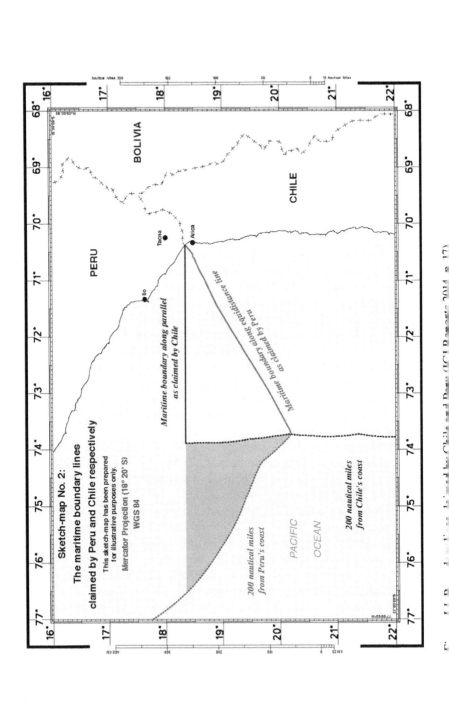

Sketch-map No. 2:
The maritime boundary lines
claimed by Peru and Chile respectively

This sketch-map has been prepared
for illustrative purposes only.
Mercator Projection (18° 20' S)
WGS 84

PERU

BOLIVIA

CHILE

Ilo

Tacna

Arica

Maritime boundary along parallel
as claimed by Chile

Maritime boundary along equidistance line
as claimed by Peru

PACIFIC
OCEAN

200 nautical miles
from Peru's coast

200 nautical miles
from Chile's coast

Frontier Agreement. Since this provision, as acknowledged by the Court, did not indicate when or by what means the tacit agreement was concluded, the Court gave content to the agreement by reference to the practice of the parties. The location of the boundary was not controversial. The Court decided by a vote of fifteen to one (Judge Sebutinde, dissenting, #198) that the boundary ran along the parallel of latitude in a seaward direction. The controversial question, however, was the extent of the boundary along the parallel. By a majority of ten to six (#198), the Court found that the extension of the tacitly agreed boundary was 80 nm, not 200 nm as proclaimed by the parties in the *Santiago Declaration*. The six judges in the minority rejected the Court's conclusion on the extent of the boundary because they did not agree with the Court's finding on the tacit agreement. Judge Sebutinde voted against because she did not believe that the parties had entered into any form of delimitation agreement. The other five judges (President Tomka and Judges Xue, Gaja, Bhandari and Orrego Vicuña) held that the instruments signed by the parties in 1952 and 1954 had delimited the lateral boundary and that its seaward extension was 200 nm. Interestingly, two of the judges who voted with the majority, Judge Sepulveda-Amor and Judge Owada, also had reservations about the existence of a tacit agreement, yet they voted with the majority as they were not persuaded that the parties had expressly delimited their lateral boundary. After determining that the seaward extension of the tacitly agreed boundary was 80 nm, the Court applied the equidistance method to delimit the remaining section of the lateral boundary (see Figure I.2).

The Court gave the parties almost half of what they had claimed. Chile, which claimed that the boundary had a 200 nm extension, was awarded a boundary line of 80 nm along the parallel of latitude. Peru, which claimed that the Court should apply the equidistance method to delimit the entire boundary, was given an equidistance line beyond the 80 nm point. This finding might suggest that the Court's objective was to split the difference so as to avoid an outcome unacceptable to the parties (Abugattás 2014; Aguayo 2014; Arnello 2014; Graham 2015; Infante 2014; Lopez Escarcena 2014; Novak and García-Corrochano 2014; Parodi 2014; Weisburd 2016:318–321). Some, who are critical of the Court's reasoning on legal grounds, believe nevertheless that the outcome was equitable. Christine Gray, for example, argues that while the Court's reasoning 'does not seem entirely coherent or compelling...the end result may well be equitable' (Gray 2015:602). Robin Churchill, who finds the Judgment intellectually unconvincing, also believes that the outcome was equitable (Churchill 2015:636).

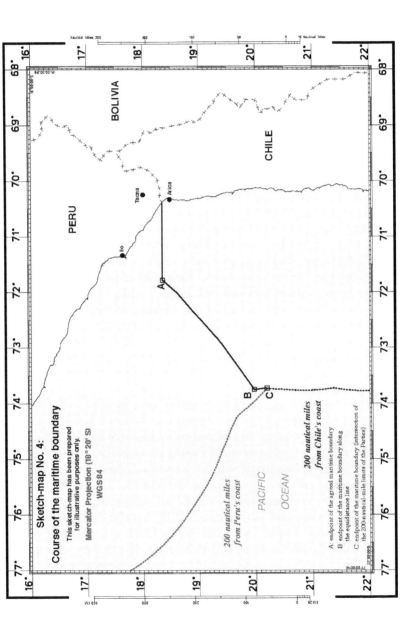

Figure I.2 Course of the maritime boundary (ICJ Reports 2014, p. 70).

These opinions, however respectable, are not reassuring. How could an outcome be seen as fair despite being incoherent or intellectually unconvincing, especially since the parties had not given the Court jurisdiction to decide the case *ex aequo et bono*? It is therefore necessary to assess this Judgment in terms of the relevant rules of international law, in particular the rules on treaty interpretation. This is the objective of this book.

The book is divided into two parts. Part I assesses the Court's approach to treaty interpretation, focusing on whether the *Santiago Declaration* delimited the maritime boundary. Part II examines the Court's finding that the parties entered into a tacit agreement and discusses the evidence and reasoning that support this finding. The book does not discuss either the delimitation carried out by the Court beyond the 80 nm point or the two additional submissions made by Peru.[1]

---

1 For a discussion on the delimitation beyond Point A see Churchill (2015:631–636); Evans (2015:260, 266–269, 272). One of Peru's additional submissions concerned the starting point of the maritime boundary. Rejecting Chile's view that the starting point of the maritime boundary was *Hito* No. 1, it argued that the correct starting point was point Concordia, located about 150 meters south of *Hito* No. 1. On this point the Court held that, on the basis of an understanding between the parties, dating back to 1968, the starting point of the maritime boundary was *Hito* No. 1 (##175, 176). Peru also argued that it was entitled to exercise sovereign rights over a maritime area lying within 200 nm of its own coast, but beyond 200 nm from the Chilean coast. The Court did not rule on this second submission because as a result of the equidistance line drawn by the Court the area claimed by Peru became part of its exclusive economic zone (##188/189).

Part I

The Santiago Declaration and connected treaties

This Part examines the Court's approach to the interpretation of the *Santiago Declaration* and its connected treaties. It provides background information on the *Declaration* and the network of treaties that form part of its context. It identifies the main weaknesses in the Court's reasoning and offers an account of the object and purpose of the *Declaration* and of the Agreements that are part of its context. It also includes a comprehensive account of the development of Paragraph IV of the *Declaration* and an examination of the relevant Minutes. This Part argues that a correct application of the international customary principles of treaty interpretation shows that the parties' understanding was that they had delimited the entire lateral boundary when they concluded the *Declaration*. It also considers why neither the judges who disagreed with the Court's finding nor Chile, which argued that the parties had delimited the entire lateral boundary, offered a persuasive alternative to the Court's reasoning. The final remark raises concerns about the Court's failure to respond to some of the arguments presented by the parties.

A. Background

Between 1952 and 1954, Chile, Ecuador and Peru (hereafter 'CEP countries') held two Conferences on the Exploitation and Conservation of the Marine Resources of the South Pacific and concluded ten legal instruments: four in 1952 at the Conference in Santiago and six in 1954 at the Conference in Lima (Annex 4). The most important was the *Santiago Declaration on the Maritime Zone* (hitherto *Santiago Declaration*) (Annex 1), which proclaims the parties' sovereignty and jurisdiction over 200 nautical miles (hitherto nm) from their coasts, including the sea floor and subsoil. Prior to the *Declaration*, Chile and Peru had issued separate, but concordant Unilateral Proclamations claiming sovereignty and jurisdiction over the adjacent sea up to a distance of 200 nm from the coast. The Proclamations were direct antecedents of the 1952 claim. Nevertheless, during the litigation the parties agreed that their Proclamations had not implicitly delimited their lateral boundary (#39).[1]

The maritime claim of the CEP countries was comprehensive. It covered an area of the sea extending 200 nm from their coasts and included living and non-living marine resources in the continental shelf and the subsoil. The *Declaration* was careful to state that CEP countries would respect the rights of third parties, mainly free navigation, and would implement adequate conservation measures to protect the marine environment and its resources. This reassurance did not satisfy the leading maritime nations, in particular the United States and the United Kingdom, which regarded this vast area of the South Pacific as part of the high seas where their whale hunting and fishing fleets could operate without restriction (there were also protests from Denmark, Norway and Sweden, CCM Annexes 60, 62, 63, 64, 65, 68). They thus promptly issued diplomatic protests, setting the stage for a protracted political and diplomatic dispute between the CEP countries and the United States and other leading maritime nations (Bayitch 1956:499; Kunz 1956:10, 836; Loring 1971:401; Selak 1950:674; Waldock 1956:193; Weissberg 1967:715; Young 1951:2386).

The 200 nm claim, though novel and wide-ranging, was part of a broader process of change in the law of the sea, prompted by major advances in naval and merchant shipping and the emergence of new technologies in fishing and mineral exploitation. In response to these developments, numerous countries made claims that challenged established legal doctrine and international security. As Whittemore Boggs noted in 1951 (Boggs 1951:185):

> Never have national claims in adjacent seas been so numerous, so varied, or so inconsistent. And never, for nations facing the high seas, has there been so great a need for universally accepted specific limits of the areas under their jurisdiction in the waters, the

---

1   Peru's Proclamation stated that it exercised control and protection 'on the seas adjacent to the Peruvian coast over the area covered between the coast and an imaginary parallel line to it at a distance of two hundred (200) nautical miles measured following the line of the geographical parallels'. Chile's Proclamation provided that its maritime zone was 'within the perimeter formed by the coast and the mathematical parallel projected into the sea at a distance of 200 nautical miles from the coasts of Chilean territory'.

sea bed, and the air space adjacent to their coasts. Unless a resolute effort is made to master this situation, it can readily lead to increasing international friction.

The Truman Proclamations of 1945 were the trigger for the flood of claims seeking to enclose maritime areas within nation state jurisdiction (Borchard 1946:55; Francois 1955:81; Hollick 1978:80; Krueger and Nordquist 1979:326; Young 1949). President Truman claimed jurisdiction and control over the continental shelf and announced the establishment of conservation protection zones in areas where vessels from the United States had traditionally fished, regardless of the distance from its coast (Bishop 1962:1212–1213; Hollick 1977–1976; US Naval War College 1956:434). The Truman Proclamations prompted Chile and Peru in 1947 to issue separate proclamations claiming sovereignty and control over the sea adjacent to their coasts to a distance of 200 nm miles and over the continental shelf (Martens 1976:533). Although the US and the Chile/Peru claims were both unilateral acts of appropriation, they were met by markedly different responses. The United States' claim to the continental shelf, which involved assuming sovereign control over 760,000 square miles of submerged land, carefully avoided using the word sovereignty. Yet, the scope of the claim was such that in 1945 the US Secretary of the Interior described it as equivalent to the opening of the American West or the acquisition of Alaska (US Naval War College 1959/60:34). Despite the enormous area covered by the US claim, other leading maritime powers raised no objections. Their response to the claim by the CEP countries was altogether different. Both the US and the UK Governments rejected it on the ground that it was in breach of the established rule that the territorial sea could not extend beyond 3 miles from the coast. At the time, however, the 3-mile rule was not universally accepted, a point that was strongly made by CEP countries and confirmed by leading contemporary publicists (Bingham 1938:6; Borchard 1946:57; Gidel 1934:171–176; Lauterpacht 1955:24–25; Oda 1955:417). An interesting perspective emerges when a comparison is made between President Truman's justification and the CEP countries' justification. President Truman argued that the appropriation of the continental shelf was justified because it was essential that a country was responsible for the conservation and prudent utilization of the resources in the continental shelf. The CEP countries made a similar point. They argued that their claim was justified in order to conserve, develop and exploit marine resources critical to their economic development. While leading maritime powers and their lawyers accepted the US justification without objections, they categorically rejected the CEP countries' argument (US Naval War College 1959/60:46–50; but see Francois 1955:82). This difference was naturally prompted by different political and economic interests rather than by legal doctrine or principle (Bingham 1940). Indeed, those who agreed with the Truman argument that the search for oil and mineral resources by US companies would further the cause of humanity, did not agree with the CEP countries' claim because they did not believe that they were honest or capable of making good use of the resources of the sea. (Goldie 1969:31; Kunz 1956:838).

The CEP countries argued that it was indispensable to consider both environmental and economic development factors in order to protect the maritime resources adjacent to their coasts. This point was eloquently made by Enrique García-Sayán, Foreign Minister and member of Peru's delegation to the First Law of the Sea Conference. In his statement to the Conference, Mr. García-Sayán noted that the Humboldt Current, which has a mean width of 200 nm, was crucially important, accounting for a large concentration of fish, and so providing a valuable source of food for humans and, indirectly, fertilizers for agriculture. He also noted that the current has the effect of preventing cloud formation, thus making the area off the Peruvian coast extremely arid, thus underlying the connection between marine conditions and living organisms in adjoining lands. Thus, in his view, the 200 nm claim constituted a biological limit, essential to promoting well-balanced development (United Nations Conference on the Law of the Sea 1958, Volume IV:17–18; see also, García-Sayán 1974). In technical terms, the CEP countries argued that the extension of their sovereignty had the purpose of defending the 'bioma' (or biome), that the biological communities established as a consequence of common climate conditions (US Department of State 1955:1029; US Department of State (Mimeo) 1955:30–32). This argument was an early formulation of the ecosystem perspective reflected in the Rio Declaration (Principle 7) and in environmental treaties such as the *Convention on Biological Diversity*, which defines an ecosystem as 'a dynamic complex of plant, animal and micro-organism communities and their non-living environment interacting as a functional unit'(See, Matz-Lück and Fuchs 2015:512–513). At the time, however, the CEP countries' argument was swiftly dismissed by the United States and even ridiculed by some commentators (Goldie 1969). The prevailing view at the time was that the resources of the sea were inexhaustible and that any attempt to restrict distant fishing fleets from exploiting resources adjacent to the CEP countries' coast was a breach of international law. As the materials in Part II of this book show, this negative response was not shared by most countries in the Latin American region or by smaller coastal countries in other parts of the world. The hostile response of the leading maritime powers did not, however, undermine the CEP countries' resolve to pursue it. The three Law of the Sea Conferences of 1958, 1960 and 1974 provided them with an important platform to seek international support for their claim. Their efforts were rewarded when, in 1982, the Third Law of the Sea Conference established the Exclusive Economic Zone (EEZ) of no more than 200 nm as a recognised maritime zone. The CEP countries took credit and were given credit for their contribution to the development of the law of the sea (Fleischer 1988:124; Zacklin 1974:62). In a letter to the President of the Conference, dated 28 April 1982, they expressed their delight, noting that

> the universal recognition of the rights of sovereignty and jurisdiction of the coastal State within the 200-mile limit provided for in the draft convention is a fundamental achievement of the countries members of the Permanent Commission of the South Pacific, in accordance with the basic objectives stated in the Santiago Declaration of 1952 issued by the Diplomatic Conference on the Exploitation and Conservation of the Marine Resources of the South Pacific held by Chile, Ecuador, and Peru.
> (A/CONF.62/L.143, *Third United Nations Conference on the Law of the Sea*, 1973–1982, Vol. XVI, Eleventh Session)

The international recognition of the EEZ was, however, a mixed blessing. It eroded the solidarity among CEP countries and encouraged Peru openly to question whether the *Santiago Declaration* had settled its maritime boundary with Chile. This was a surprising development since for nearly four decades the CEP countries seemed to agree that their lateral boundary was the geographic parallel starting from the land boundary terminus and extending seaward to a distance of 200 nm. This view was also reflected in numerous authoritative publications and statements by Government officials from third countries, international lawyers and international institutions (Jagota 1981:118; Oxman 1994:260–261; Prescott and Schoffield 2005:231; United Nations 2000:58; US State Department 1979; for additional references see CCM:155–173). The most authoritative acknowledgement of the delimitation is contained in a special report by Eduardo Jiménez de Aréchaga, a widely respected international lawyer and former member and President of the International Court of Justice (Jiménez de Aréchaga 1993). In 1986, however, Peru challenged this understanding.

In a letter to the Chilean Foreign Minister, Peru requested a definitive and comprehensive delimitation of the lateral maritime boundaries. Although Chile's response was strangely evasive, there were no immediate consequences, and Peru did not pursue this question until 2001. There then followed a series of unsuccessful diplomatic exchanges until 2008, when Peru formally requested the ICJ to delimit its lateral maritime boundary. Chile did not contest the Court's jurisdiction, but claimed that the *Santiago Declaration* had delimited the lateral boundary between the two countries. The Court delivered its judgment in January 2014.

B. Overview: approach to treaty interpretation

This Section highlights the four main weaknesses of the Court's interpretation of the *Santiago Declaration*: its reliance on a literal approach to the interpretation of Paragraph IV; its inadequate analysis of the *Declaration*; its failure to take the context into account and its disregard of the practice of the parties.

1. Literal meaning

The *Santiago Declaration* of 1952 sets out the CEP countries' maritime claim. Paragraph IV, its delimitation provision, reads as follow:

> In the case of island territories, the zone of 200 nautical miles shall apply to the entire coast of the island or group of islands. If an island or group of islands belonging to one of the countries making the declaration is less than 200 nautical miles from the general maritime zone belonging to another of those countries, the maritime zone of the island or group of islands shall be limited by the parallel at the point at which the land frontier of the States concerned reaches the sea.

The parties had different views on the meaning of this provision. Peru, claiming that the lateral boundary between Chile and Peru had never been delimited, argued that the second sentence of Paragraph IV applied only to islands in the Ecuador-Peru border, as there were no islands in the vicinity of the land boundary between Chile and Peru (PM:130,132). Its objective was to limit an island's 200 nm maritime zone in the event it overlapped with the maritime zones generated by the continental coast. Paragraph IV, according to Peru, could not have delimited the parties' entire lateral boundary because, at the time, international law did not recognise the parties' claim (PR:144–145,158). Peru also noted that the 200 nm claim did not require any form of delimitation because it was merely a functional device aimed at protecting the parties' fishing resources (PM:98).

Chile argued that Paragraph IV had delimited the parties' entire lateral boundary. According to Chile, the reference to the parallel in the second sentence presupposed that the lateral boundary had been delimited by the parallel. It argued that unless the entire lateral boundary had been delimited it would not be possible to determine whether an island is located less than 200 nm from the general maritime zone of a neighbouring state (CCM:83). Chile also argued that the text of the *Special Agreement* of 1954 and numerous exchanges between the parties recorded in the Minutes of the *Declaration* and its connected Agreements supported its interpretation. Chile did not concede that Paragraph IV was ambiguous.

The Court's interpretation of Paragraph IV focused exclusively on the text's literal meaning (#60):

> The Court turns now to paragraph IV of the 1952 Santiago Declaration. The first sentence of paragraph IV specifies that the proclaimed 200-nautical-mile maritime zones apply also in the case of island territories. The second sentence of that paragraph addresses the situation where an island or group of islands of one State party is located less than 200 nautical miles from the general maritime zone of another State party. In this situation, the limit of the respective zones shall be the parallel at the point at which the land frontier of the State concerned reaches the sea. The Court observes that this provision, the only one in the 1952 Santiago Declaration making any reference to the limits of the States parties' maritime zones, is silent regarding the lateral limits of the maritime zones which are not derived from island territories and which do not abut them.

The Court agreed with Peru's main argument that Paragraph IV only applies to islands and that the lateral boundary had not been delimited. As a consequence, since there are no islands in the vicinity of the Chile/Peru boundary, Paragraph IV did not apply to Chile.

The Court unequivocally rejected Chile's argument. Its reasoning was as follows (#61):

> The Court is not convinced by Chile's argument that paragraph IV can be understood solely if it is considered to delimit not

only insular maritime zones but also the entirety of the general maritime zones of the States parties. The ordinary meaning of paragraph IV reveals a particular interest in the maritime zones of islands which may be relevant even if a general maritime zone has not yet been established. In effect, it appears that the States parties intended to resolve a specific issue which could obviously create possible future tension between them by agreeing that the parallel would limit insular zones.

After dismissing Chile's argument the Court restated its main finding, employing the language of the customary rules of treaty interpretation (#62):

> In light of the foregoing, the Court concludes that the ordinary meaning of paragraph IV, read in its context, goes no further than establishing the Parties' agreement concerning the limits between certain insular maritime zones and those zones generated by the continental coasts which abut such insular maritime zones.

2. *Inadequate analysis of the Santiago Declaration*

The Court's analysis of the *Declaration* pays little attention to its object and purpose. Instead, it is dominated by the single objective of finding the delimitation clause. It begins with two telling statements. First, it queries whether the *Declaration* can be regarded as a delimitation treaty, since it does not contain an 'express reference' to the delimitation of maritime boundaries of the zones generated by the continental coasts of the parties. Secondly, it observes that the *Declaration* does not contain the type of information 'expected in an agreement determining maritime boundaries, namely, specific co-ordinates or cartographic material' (#58). The first observation merely anticipates the Court's main finding and the second is misleading because it assumes, incorrectly, that when the *Declaration* was drafted there was a well-established practice on maritime delimitation. Indeed, before 1952 only very few maritime delimitation agreements had been concluded and there was no uniform practice regarding the technical information contained in these agreements (Prescott and Schoffield 2005:1). More importantly, however, this observation contradicts the finding that Paragraph IV of the *Declaration* had delimited the maritime zones of islands (#62).

After some brief comments on Paragraphs II, III and VI the Court concludes that none presupposes that the lateral boundary had been delimited. According to the Court, Paragraph II, which proclaims the parties' seaward claim stating that each party 'possesses exclusive sovereignty and jurisdiction over the sea along the coasts of their respective countries to a minimum distance of 200 nautical miles', makes no reference to the need to establish lateral limits (#59). Likewise, the Court observes that the reference in Paragraph III to the parties' sovereignty and jurisdiction over the seabed and subsoil does not imply any form of delimitation (#59). The relevance of these observations is questionable since it would be unreasonable to expect all the provisions of the *Declaration* explicitly to refer to the delimitation of the lateral boundaries. The Court also examined Paragraph VI, which conveys the parties' intention to establish norms to regulate activities in their respective maritime zones. Its comments on this Paragraph reveal a remarkable lack of interest in ascertaining the nature and purpose of the *Declaration* (#59):

> Paragraph VI expresses the intention of the States parties to establish by agreement in the future general norms of regulation and protection to be applied in their respective maritime zones. Accordingly, although a description of the distance of maritime zones and reference to the exercise of jurisdiction and sovereignty might indicate that the States parties were not unaware of issues of general delimitation, the Court concludes that neither paragraph II nor paragraph III refers explicitly to any lateral boundaries of the proclaimed 200-nautical-mile maritime zones, nor can the need for such boundaries be implied by the references to jurisdiction and sovereignty.

This brief and inadequate analysis of the *Declaration* leads the Court to conclude that Paragraph IV is only concerned with the delimitation of the maritime zones of islands (#60). This finding is not supported by either a careful analysis of the drafting history of Paragraph IV or a comprehensive examination of the object and purpose of the *Declaration*.

3. Disregard of context

The Agreements concluded by the parties in Lima in 1954 are critically important. They are context for the purpose of determining the ordinary meaning of Paragraph IV because they are legally connected to the *Declaration*. The Court, however, considered these Agreements as self-contained instruments, not directly related to the *Declaration*.

In Section IV(3) of the Judgment, the Court describes them as 'the various 1954 Agreements'. This characterisation suggests a deliberate attempt to undervalue their legal significance.

(a) A note on context

The Court applied the customary rules of treaty interpretation, as reflected in the Vienna Convention on the Law of Treaties (VCLT) (#57). In an earlier case, the Court provided a helpful summary of these rules (*Territorial Dispute Libyan Jamahirija/Chad,* Judgment, I.C.J. Reports 1994, 6 at 21):

> The Court would recall that, in accordance with customary international law, reflected in Article 31 of the 1969 Vienna Convention on the Law of Treaties, a treaty must be interpreted in good faith in accordance with the ordinary meaning to be given to its terms in their context and in the light of its object and purpose. Interpretation must be based above all upon the text of the treaty. As a supplementary measure recourse may be had to means of interpretation such as the preparatory work of the treaty and the circumstances of its conclusion.

It is generally acknowledged that the task of the interpreter under VCLT rules is to elucidate the meaning of the terms of the treaty, rather than immediately to engage in an investigation of the intention of the parties. This is so because the text of the treaty is regarded as the authentic expression of the intention of the parties (YILC 1966 (II):220). The meaning of the text of the treaty, however, is not determined exclusively by the rules of language. This is why VCLT rules provide that the ordinary meaning of the terms of the treaty emerges from the context in which they are used and in the context of the treaty as a whole. Indeed, such is the importance of the context in determining the ordinary meaning that when the VCLT was drafted some members of the International Law Commission (ILC) considered that Article 31(4) was superfluous. This provision states that 'a special meaning shall be given to a term if it is established that the parties so intended'. The Commissioners who deemed this provision superfluous argued that the so-called special meaning would always be the natural meaning in the particular context (*United Nations Conference on the Law of Treaties* 1968 (Waldock:184).

Context comprises the entire text of the treaty, agreements 'made between all the parties in connection with the conclusion of the treaty'

(VCLT, Article 31(2)(a)) and instruments 'made by one or more parties in connection with the conclusion of the treaty and accepted by the other parties as an instrument related to the treaty' (Article 31(2)(b)). A question arising from Article 31(2)(a) is when should such agreements be regarded as connected to the treaty? Sir Humphrey Waldock addressed this question in his 1964 Report to the ILC. He noted that instruments connected or related to the treaty are not automatically considered to be an integral part of the treaty. In his view, 'whether they are an actual part of the treaty depends on the intention of the parties in each case' (YILC1964 (II):58). He then went on to explain the significance of connected treaties for the purpose of interpretation. In his view, these agreements

> should not be regarded as mere evidence to which recourse may be had for the purpose of resolving an ambiguity or obscurity but as part of the context for the purpose of arriving at the natural and ordinary meaning of the terms of the treaty.
>
> (YILC1964 (II):58)

Connected agreements of the type envisaged under Article 31(2) of the VCLT are not a supplementary means of interpretation. On the contrary, they are essential components in the determination of the ordinary meaning of the terms of the treaty. Cases where connected agreements were considered context include the *Ambatielos case* (I.C.J. Reports 1952, 28 at 43, 75) and the *Territorial Dispute Libyan Jamahirija/Chad* (I.C.J. Reports 1994, 6, paragraphs 37 and 53). In the *Diversion of Water from the River Meuse*, the Permanent Court of International Justice held that there was no juridical connection between three agreements concluded and ratified on the same day (*Diversion of Water from the River Meuse, Netherlands v. Belgium,* Judgment, 1937, PCIJ, Series A/B, No. 70, 4, paragraph 34).

The VCLT does not specify the time within which agreements made 'in connection with the conclusion of the treaty' should be concluded. This question is discussed by Sir Robert Jennings and Sir Arthur Watts in the ninth edition of *Oppenheim's International Law*. Their view is that the phrase employed in the VCLT, 'in connection with the conclusion of the treaty' is not the same as at the time of the conclusion of the treaty, provided that the period—before or after—the original and the connected agreement is not excessively long. They also note that connected agreements are often part of a network of treaties which 'can be viewed together as a whole' (*Oppenheim's International Law* 1992:1274; see also Villiger 2009:429–430; Yasseen 1976:38).

(b) The standard clause in the Lima Agreements

The 1954 Agreements were not, as the Court's depiction suggests, random agreements. They are legally connected to the *Declaration,* and, as such, part of the context for the purpose of its interpretation. The parties concluded ten connected Agreements in two successive conferences bearing the same name: *Conference on the Exploitation and Conservation of the Maritime Resources of the South Pacific.* Four of these agreements were concluded in 1952 at the Santiago Conference and six in 1954 at the Lima Conference (Annex No. 4). The close connection between the four Santiago Agreements and the six Lima Agreements is underscored by a standard clause, included in all the instruments adopted in Lima, which reads as follow:

> All the provisions of this Agreement shall be deemed to be an integral and supplementary part of, and not in any way to abrogate, the resolutions and decisions adopted at the Conference on the Exploitation and Conservation of the Maritime Resources of the South Pacific, held in Santiago de Chile in August 1952.

The standard clause confirms that the parties' intention was to regard the Agreements concluded in Santiago in 1952 and in Lima in 1954 as connected treaties. The objective of these Agreements was to establish a coherent and comprehensive legal framework to control and regulate activities within the maritime zones covered by their claim. Since the Agreements were 'made between all the parties in connection with the conclusion of the treaty' (VCLT, Article 31(2)(a)), they are part of the context for the purpose of determining the ordinary meaning of Paragraph IV. Moreover, because the period between the adoption of the Lima Agreements and the *Declaration* is only two years, these Agreements should be regarded as connected to the *Santiago Declaration* (*Oppenheim's International Law* 1992:1274).

The Court, however, did not interpret the standard clause as having connected the Lima Agreements to the Agreements concluded in Santiago. It dismissed it on the ground that the clause was added 'late in the drafting process without any explanation recorded in the Minutes' (#73). The Court's dismissal is surprising because this clause—not unlike a clause in a treaty interpreted by the Permanent Court of International Justice (PCIJ) in 1923—'leaves little to be desired in the nature of clearness' (*Acquisition of Polish Nationality, Advisory Opinion,* 1923, P.C. I. J., Series B, No. 7, p. 20.). The Court's refusal to give effect to this straightforward provision is also ironic because its observation indicates that, while it took the time to examine the Minutes of the Lima Conference to explain why it would disregard the standard clause, it failed to take any notice of information contained in the same Minutes which, as I explain below, demonstrate that the *Declaration* had delimited the entire lateral boundary.

4. Disregard of the practice of the parties

According to the Court, Paragraph IV only delimited the maritime zone of islands in the event that they overlapped with the general maritime zones generated by the continent. The implication of this finding is that Paragraph IV did not apply to Chile because there are no relevant islands in the vicinity of the boundary between Chile and Peru. It also suggests that while the CEP countries had carefully designed a comprehensive regulatory framework to protect and manage their claim, they had failed to delimit their entire lateral boundaries and, instead, had chosen to focus on a segment of the boundary, relevant only to a tiny portion of the lateral boundary between Peru and Ecuador.

Since the *Santiago Declaration* had been in force for more than half a century, an examination of the practice of the parties would have enabled the Court to test the soundness of its finding. The parties, of course, discussed their practice in great detail. Chile argued that, in their practice, both parties had acknowledged that Paragraph IV of the *Declaration* had delimited the entire lateral boundary. The practice invoked by Chile included numerous exchanges between the parties; diplomatic exchanges with third parties; acts of jurisdiction by the parties within their respective maritime zones; and internal correspondence and statements by senior officials confirming their understanding regarding the location of the boundary. Peru vigorously, and in great detail, challenged the evidence submitted by Chile. Its main argument, however, was that subsequent practice was irrelevant because international law would not have allowed the parties to delimit maritime zones that had not been universally recognised.

The Court—with the exception of the Lighthouse Arrangements (see Section E, below)—disregarded the practice of the parties as a means of testing the soundness of its interpretation of Paragraph IV of the *Declaration*.[2] Nevertheless, it analysed in detail the practice of

---

2 The Court discusses the Lighthouse Arrangements in three subsections of the Judgment to determine three different issues: whether they provide evidence of an agreed maritime boundary (#96–99); whether they provide evidence about the extent of the lateral boundary (#130); and whether they provide an indication of the starting

the parties in order to ascertain whether it revealed anything about the extent of the lateral boundary (#119–142). The Court, however, failed to find in these materials any explicit reference to the extent of the boundary. This outcome was predictable because the parties were not concerned with the extension of the boundary: Chile because it assumed that if the Court found that Paragraph IV had delimited the boundary its extension would be 200 nm; Peru because it did not accept that Paragraph IV of the *Declaration* applied to the Chile/Peru boundary. Thus, the evidence submitted by the parties was not concerned with the extension of the boundary.

Although the Court was unable to find any information on the extent of the boundary in the evidence on subsequent practice, it is interesting to examine how it responded to two events cited by Chile as relevant practice: the *Accession Protocol to the Santiago Declaration* and the negotiations between Chile and Bolivia on Bolivia's access to the sea.

(a) The Accession Protocol

In 1955 the CEP countries concluded an *Accession Protocol to the Santiago Declaration* to encourage other Latin American countries to accept the *Declaration* and thus strengthen their maritime claim on the international plane. The *Protocol*, however, excluded Paragraph IV of the *Declaration* and instead inserted a provision stating that

> each State may determine the extension and manner of delimitation of its respective zone, with respect to part or the entirety of its shoreline, in accordance with its distinctive geographic reality, the magnitude of each sea, and the geological and biological factors conditioning the existence, conservation and development of maritime flora and fauna in its waters.
>
> (PM: Annex 52)

Chile argued that the exclusion of Paragraph IV from the *Accession Protocol* was an acknowledgement by the three parties that this provision had delimited their lateral boundaries (CCM:240–242).

---

point of the lateral boundary (#152–176). On the first issue, the Court concludes that, while the Lighthouse Arrangements show that there was a lateral boundary beyond 12 nm, they do not provide evidence of a pre-existent delimitation. On the second issue, the Court found that the Lighthouse Arrangements did not provide any information about the extent of the lateral boundary. On the third question, the Court concludes that the Lighthouse Arrangements support the conclusion that the starting point of the boundary is Boundary Marker No. 1 (*Hito* No. 1).

Chile supported its argument with reference to the preparatory work of the *Accession Protocol*. During the negotiations, Chile and Peru sent separate Notes to Ecuador, which was in charge of drafting the document, pointing out that while Paragraph IV of the *Declaration* had delimited the boundaries of the CEP countries, the method employed by this provision was not necessarily applicable elsewhere (CCM: Annex 70 and Annex 71).

The Court's response to Chile's argument was as follows: 'Given the conclusion that the Court has already reached on paragraph IV... the Court does not see the Protocol as having any real significance' (#125). The Court reached this conclusion without taking into account the exchange of notes between the parties. The form of words it uses to reject Chile's argument is revealing, suggesting, as it does, that the subsequent practice of the parties cannot contradict its interpretation of Paragraph IV.

(b) Negotiations with Bolivia

The Court also dismissed, as irrelevant to the interpretation of Paragraph IV, the evidence on the negotiations between Chile and Bolivia in 1975/76. The negotiations concerned Bolivia's access to the sea. Under the Chile-Peru Treaty of Lima of 1929, any cession or exchange of territory to Bolivia would have required Peru's consent. The terms of the proposed cession included land territory and a 5.1 mile wide maritime zone bounded by two parallels extending for 200 nm along the existing lateral boundary. Peru was consulted and raised no objections to the proposed maritime boundary, but did raise questions about the cession of land territory. In the event, however, the negotiations between Chile and Bolivia did not succeed. Chile argued that Peru's lack of response confirmed that it acknowledged that the lateral boundary between the two countries ran seaward along the parallel passing through Boundary Marker No. 1. In other words, Peru had acknowledged that the lateral boundary had been delimited by Paragraph IV of the *Santiago Declaration*.

The Court did not consider these negotiations as relevant to the issue concerning the extent of the lateral boundary. It also made some general comments about the negotiations (#133):

> The Court does not find these negotiations significant for the issue of the extent of the maritime boundary between the Parties. While Chile's proposal referred to the territorial sea, economic zone and continental shelf, Peru did not accept this proposal. Peru's

January 1976 acknowledgment did not mention any existing maritime boundary between the Parties, while its counter-proposal from November of that year did not indicate the extent or nature of the maritime area proposed to be accorded to Bolivia.

The Court's comments are sketchy. They highlight that Peru did not accept the proposal submitted by Chile in January 1976, but do not take into account that Peru's objection was over the territorial status of Arica and Tacna, not about the cession of maritime territory. Its hurried response to the evidence demonstrates, yet again, the Court's unwillingness to consider facts that might have challenged the accuracy of its interpretation of Paragraph IV of the *Declaration*.

C. Object, purpose and context

1. In general

This section examines the context, object and purpose of the *Santiago Declaration* and its connected treaties. The *Declaration*, the three Agreements concluded in Santiago in 1952 and the six Agreements concluded in Lima in 1954 are connected agreements that complement and reinforce each other. Together, they define the scope of the parties' maritime claim, establish rules to regulate activities by its citizens and by foreign nationals in their respective maritime zones and provide a formal structure to secure the parties' commitment to defend and attract international support for their claim.

2. The Santiago Declaration

The main objective of the *Santiago Declaration* was to establish the parties' maritime claim of 200 nm (Annex 1). It is a short document of six paragraphs: the first paragraph states that the prevailing notions on breadth of the territorial sea and contiguous zone are inadequate for the conservation and development of marine flora and fauna along their coast; the second and third paragraphs set out the parties' claim to sovereignty and jurisdiction over the sea, up to a minimum distance of 200 nm, including the sea along their coasts, the seabed and subsoil thereof; the fourth paragraph is the important, but controversial delimitation provision; the fifth paragraph provides that the *Declaration* respects the right of innocent passage in accordance with international law; and the sixth paragraph announces the parties' intention to enter into agreements to regulate activities in their respective maritime zones and in areas of common interest.

that the parties shall enforce the agreements concluded at the Santiago Conference and apply penalties for breaches committed within their jurisdiction (Comisión Permanente del Pacífico Sur 2007:59; US Naval War College 1956:267). The notion that each of the three parties to the *Declaration* had exclusive jurisdiction within their respective maritime zones was confirmed two years later, at the Lima Conference, when the parties entered into a series of linked agreements designed to protect hunting and fishing within their respective maritime zones and regulate the exploitation of other resources in the area.

3. The 1954 Lima Agreements

Two years after signing the *Santiago Declaration*, the CEP countries held the *Second Conference on the Exploitation and Conservation of the Marine Resources of the South Pacific*, in Lima, and concluded six Agreements (Annex 4). The Conference had two main objectives: (1) to reaffirm the parties' commitment to the defence of their 200 nm claim, which had come under strong criticism by the world's leading maritime powers; and (2) to establish norms to regulate and protect activities and resources in their respective maritime zones. The most important agreement was the *Complementary Convention to the Declaration of Sovereignty over the Maritime Zone of Two Hundred Miles* (herewith *Complementary Convention*) (Annex 2). It reaffirms the parties' claim and sets out a series of measures to safeguard and defend it. Also, it unambiguously affirms that the three states have distinct and well-defined maritime zones and enjoins the parties from concluding 'any agreements, arrangements or conventions which imply a diminution of the sovereignty over the said zone' (Article 4). The notion that each state has sovereignty over a distinct and well-defined maritime zone is highlighted by Article 3, which provides that in the event of a de facto violation of the maritime zone of any of the three states, the state that suffers such violation shall communicate this event to the other two states 'for the purpose of determining what action should be taken to safeguard the sovereignty which has been violated'. The Court acknowledged that the *Complementary Convention* was the most important agreement concluded in Lima, but, disappointingly, its analysis is brief and incomplete. It mentions the purpose of the Convention and makes an obscure comment as to whether the 'primary purpose' of this Convention determined the outcome of the Lima Conference: 'It does not follow, however, that the "primary purpose" was the sole purpose or even less that the primary purpose determined the sole outcome of the 1954 meeting and the Inter-State Conference' (#77).

The notion that the CEP countries had separate maritime zones of 200 nm is restated in the other agreements concluded in Lima. Article 1 of the *Convention on the Granting of Permits for the Exploitation of the Resources of the South Pacific* provides that no person can carry out maritime hunting or fishing activities within the maritime zone without a permit granted by the 'respective country', in accordance with the quotas set by the Permanent Commission (Article 2(2)). The reference to 'zones' in the title of the *Convention on Measures and Surveillance and Control of the Maritime Zones of the Signatory Countries* implies that the three maritime zones are distinct and well-defined. Article 1 provides that each signatory is responsible for controlling the exploitation of its own maritime zone (*su zona maritima*). Article 2 clarifies that each country has exclusive jurisdiction to enforce measures of surveillance and control within their respective maritime zone. The *Convention on the System of Sanctions* confirms the exclusive jurisdiction of each signatory within its maritime zone. It provides that violation of the regulations on maritime fishing and hunting shall be tried by the courts of the country that captures the offender.

It is interesting to consider how the Court interpreted two of the Agreements concluded in Lima: the *Convention on Measures of Surveillance and Control in the Maritime Zones of the Signatory Countries* and the *Convention on the Granting of Permits for the Exploitation of the Resources of the South Pacific*. Chile argued that these Conventions reflected a common understanding that the maritime zones of the three states had been delimited as they assumed that the parties exercised sovereignty within their exclusive maritime zones (CCM:149). In support of this interpretation Chile cited two articles of the *Convention on Measures of Surveillance and Control*, which the Court transcribes in paragraph 78 of the Judgment:

> First: It shall be the function of each signatory country to supervise and control the exploitation of the resources *in its Maritime Zone* by the use of such organs and means as it considers necessary.
>
> Second: The supervision and control referred to in article one shall be exercised by each country *exclusively in the waters of its jurisdiction*.
>
> (Emphasis added by Chile)

The Court flatly rejected Chile's argument (#79):

> The Court considers that at this early stage there were at least in practice distinct maritime zones in which each of the three States

might, in terms of the 1952 Santiago Declaration, take action as indeed was exemplified by the action taken by Peru against the Onassis whaling fleet shortly before the Lima Conference; other instances of enforcement by the two Parties are discussed later. However the Agreements on Supervision and Control and on the Regulation of Permits give no indication about the location or nature of boundaries of the zones. On the matter of boundaries, the Court now turns to the 1954 Special Maritime Frontier Zone Agreement.

This paragraph calls for two observations: first, the Court's rejection of Chile's argument on the ground that the Conventions gave no indication about the location of the boundaries totally misses the point: that was not the argument presented. The argument was that these Conventions presupposed that the maritime zones had been delimited in 1952. Secondly, the observation that 'at this early stage there were at least in practice distinct maritime zones in which each of the three States might in terms of the Santiago Declaration take action' is historically and legally incorrect. It is historically incorrect because it suggests that the practice of the parties within their respective maritime zones evolved in discrete stages, but, the Court gives no indication as to what happened after the 'early stage', because there were no successive stages. Indeed, the comprehensive regulatory framework adopted in Lima was not subject to any major amendment. The Court's statement is also legally incorrect because it suggests that, in practice, the *Santiago Declaration* allocated maritime zones, but that this allocation had no legal force. Thus, it seems that, according to the Court, the hypothetical allocation made by the *Declaration* was provisional and did not create sovereign rights. This view has no basis in the *Declaration* or in the text of any of the six Agreements concluded in Lima It is also inconsistent with its own interpretation that in the case of islands Paragraph IV had made a definitive allocation of maritime zones (#60).

D. Development of Paragraph IV

1. Minutes of the Santiago Declaration

The text of Paragraph IV underwent important changes during the negotiations of the *Declaration*. These changes, prompted by a request for clarification from the Ecuadorean delegate, led to a major revision of the draft. In order to determine whether the Minutes contribute towards elucidating the meaning of Paragraph IV, it is necessary to ascertain its scope. Did it concern the whole lateral boundary or was it restricted to the maritime zones of islands? This is how the Minutes, as transcribed by the Court, record Ecuador's request for clarification (#68):

> [Mr. Fernández (Ecuador)] observed that it would be advisable to provide more clarity to article 3 [which became Paragraph IV of the final text of the 1952 *Santiago Declaration*], in order to avoid any error in the interpretation of the interference zone in the case of islands, and suggested that the declaration be drafted on the basis that the boundary line of the jurisdictional zone of each country be the respective parallel from the point at which the frontier of the countries touches or reaches the sea.
>
> (#68)

Chile argued that the request included both the location of the boundary of islands and the entire lateral boundary. Peru disagreed. The Court, agreeing with Peru, held that the request was only concerned with the boundary of the maritime zones generated by islands (#68). In order to determine whether the Court's interpretation is correct it is necessary to examine draft Article 3, which the delegate from Ecuador sought to revise.

Draft Article 3 had three objectives: first (paragraph one) to define the location of the general lateral boundary and the seaward extension of the maritime area claimed by the parties; secondly (paragraph two) to establish the principle that islands were also entitled to a 200 nm maritime zone; and thirdly (paragraph three) to resolve the problem that would arise in case the maritime zone of islands located less than 200 nm from the coast overlapped with the general maritime zone of the neighbouring state.

Draft Article 3 reads as follow (this is the text used by the Court and transcribed in paragraph 67):

> The zone indicated [in the first two draft Articles] comprises all waters within the perimeter formed by the coasts of each country and a mathematical parallel projected into the sea to 200 nautical miles away from the mainland, along the coastal fringe.
>
> In the case of island territories, the zone of 200 nautical miles will apply all around the island or island group.
>
> If an island or group of islands belonging to one of the countries making the declaration is situated less than 200 nautical miles from the general maritime zone belonging to another of

those countries, according to what has been established in the first paragraph of this article, the maritime zone of the said island or group of islands shall be limited, in the corresponding part, to the distance that separates it from the maritime zone of the other State or country.

The draft was unproblematic on two points: the seaward extension of the maritime claim and the principle that islands were entitled to a 200 nm maritime zone all around the island. The provision on the seaward extension of the claim, albeit slightly amended, was moved to Paragraph II of the *Declaration*. The provision on the maritime zone of islands became the first sentence of Paragraph IV. Draft Article 3, however, did not clearly identify the location of the lateral boundary. The first paragraph of the draft Article refers to the general maritime zone as comprising 'all waters within the perimeter formed by the coasts of each country and a mathematical parallel projected into the sea to 200 nautical miles away from the mainland', but does not specify where the lateral sides of the perimeter are located. The third paragraph was unclear for the same reason. It provided that the maritime zone of islands 'shall be limited, in the corresponding part, to the distance that separates it from the maritime zone of the other State or country', but, did not identify the location of the lateral boundary. Given that neither the first nor the third draft paragraph identified the location of the lateral boundary, it is reasonable to conclude that the request for clarification concerned both, in the words used by the Ecuadorean delegate (in bold) **'the boundary line of the jurisdictional zone of each country'** (paragraph one) and the **'interference zone in the case of islands'** (paragraph 3). In his request, the delegate from Ecuador also suggested that in both cases the text should '*be drafted on the basis that the boundary line of the jurisdictional zone of each country be the respective parallel from the point at which the frontier of the countries touches or reaches the sea*'. The view that the request for clarification was not restricted to the delimitation of the maritime zone of islands is further confirmed by the fact that the delegates from Chile and Peru were entrusted with the task of re-drafting the text. If Ecuador had been concerned with the boundary line of islands, it is unlikely that either Peru or Ecuador would have allowed Chile to play such a prominent role in resolving an issue which, according to Peru, as well as the Court (#64), would be of interest only to countries with relevant islands.

Clarifying the scope of the request for clarification does not, however, resolve the problem because the second sentence of Paragraph IV does not obviously identify the location of the general boundary. The first sentence of Paragraph IV is unproblematic. It states that the 200 nm maritime claim applies to islands: 'In the case of island territories, the zone of 200 nautical miles shall apply to the entire coast of the island or group of islands'. The second sentence identifies the cut off point in the event of an overlap between the maritime zone of islands and the maritime zone of the neighbouring state: 'the maritime zone of the island or group of islands shall be limited by the parallel at the point at which the land frontier of the States concerned reaches the sea'. This sentence, however, does not precisely define the location of the general lateral boundary. If the foregoing interpretation is correct and the request for clarification concerned both the general lateral boundary and the boundary of islands, why did the revised draft not include both? One explanation is simply that the drafters changed their minds and decided not to delimit the general lateral boundary. This interpretation, favoured by the Court, seems unreasonable because the intention of the parties, as reflected in draft Article 3 and in the parties' agreement to revise its text along the lines proposed by the delegate from Ecuador, suggests that their objective was that their entire lateral boundary should be defined by Paragraph IV. Nevertheless, the fact that the parties were aware of the flaws of draft Article 3 when they acceded to Ecuador's request does not imply, as Chile claimed (CCM:81; CR:63–64), that the revised text addressed all its failings. Chile argued, however, that the second sentence of Paragraph IV had simultaneously resolved the location of both the general lateral boundary and the maritime boundary of islands. It argued that the reference to islands in Paragraph IV was a specific application of the general rule that the parallel of latitude is the boundary of both general and insular maritime zones (CCM:82; see also CR:67). The determination of the general maritime zone is thus implicit in the text of Paragraph IV. This interpretation can be graphically represented if some words in the second sentence are redacted so as to read as follows:

If an island or group of islands belonging to one of the countries making the declaration is situated less than 200 nautical miles from **the general maritime zone** belonging to another of those countries, the maritime zone of the island or group of islands **shall be limited by the parallel at the point at which the land frontier of the States concerned reaches the sea.**

At the Oral Hearings, Chile made another attempt to explain why Paragraph IV had not addressed the question of the general boundary. It began, mistakenly in my view, by denying that paragraph one of draft Article 3 was ambiguous and then went on to argue that the only remaining uncertainty concerned the location of the boundary in the case of overlap between the maritime zones of islands and the general maritime zone of the neighbouring state. The argument then proceeded as follows (*Compte Rendu* 2012/35:16 (Crawford)).

> The first paragraph of old Article III, establishing that the general maritime zones were measured, and given a perimeter, by the mathematical parallel, was deleted. But this did not involve any change in legal intent or effect. The important element was taken from the first paragraph of the draft and added to the last sentence of the final text of what became Article IV. That element was that the lateral component of the perimeter of the maritime zones, insular and general, was 'the parallel at the point at which the land frontier of the States concerned reaches the sea'. That was the maritime boundary, and that is why Article IV looks the way it does.

The notion that the deletion of the first paragraph of draft Article 3 did not involve a change in legal intent or effect begs the question. Whether or not this paragraph was unclear, its deletion hardly implies that the parties had not changed their mind. The four judges who filed a Joint Dissent—Judges Xue, Gaja, Bhandari and ad hoc Judge Orrego Vicuña—made a similar point. While accepting Chile's argument that the second sentence of Paragraph IV presupposed that the whole boundary had been delimited, they also gave weight to the fact that the agreement to revise the text revealed the parties' intention to state that the entire lateral boundary was formed by the parallel. Although they conceded that 'this view was reflected only in part in the final text', they argued that 'there is no indication in the preparatory work that the negotiators had changed their view on the boundary running between the maritime zones generated by the respective continental coasts' (Joint Dissent #8). The point, however, is not whether the parties changed their mind, but whether there is evidence that, when the signatories approved the revised text, they did so on the understanding that they were delimiting the entire lateral boundary. The Minutes of the Santiago Conference do not provide sufficient evidence that this was the case. As a consequence, they do not contradict the Court's finding that Paragraph IV was only concerned with the delimitation of the maritime zone of islands.

The interpretation of Paragraph IV, however, does not conclude at this point. In order to determine the ordinary meaning of Paragraph IV it is necessary to consider the Agreements concluded in Lima in 1954, which, by virtue of the standard clause and in accordance with Article 31(2)(a) of the VCLT are connected to the *Santiago Declaration* and therefore part of its context.

2. *Minutes of the Complementary Convention*

The Minutes of the *Complementary Convention* provide compelling evidence that when the parties concluded the *Santiago Declaration* their understanding was that Paragraph IV had delimited the entire lateral boundary. The Court, however, disregarded the Minutes as it was only interested in determining whether any of the provisions of the *Complementary Convention* had delimited the lateral boundary (#77). The Minutes explain, however, why the Convention did not include any reference to the lateral boundary and show that when the parties approved the text of Paragraph IV their understanding was that it had delimited the entire lateral boundary. The Court, though, took no notice of the Minutes (#77).

The Delegate of Ecuador, Mr. Salvador Lara, proposed that the Convention should include an additional article 'to clarify the concept of the dividing line of the jurisdictional sea, already set forth at the Santiago Conference, but which would not be redundant to reiterate here' [que aclare que el concepto de la línea divisoria del mar jurisdiccional que ya ha sido expuesto en la Conferencia de Santiago, pero que no está demás repetir aquí] (Minutes 1954 First Session). Chile and Peru did not accede to Mr. Lara's request because, in their view, Paragraph IV of the *Santiago Declaration* was very clear (*bastante claro*). [Los Señores Llosa [Perú] y Cruz-Ocampo [Chile] creen que el Artículo 4 de la Declaración de Santiago es ya bastante claro y que no cabe nueva exposición]. Since Mr. Lara insisted, the Chair of that session—who was the Chilean delegate—asked him whether, instead of adding a new article, he would be happy for the Minutes to record his speech. [...el Señor Presidente propone al Señor Delegado de Ecuador si aceptaría que en vez de un nuevo artículo se dejara constancia expresa de sus palabras en el Acta]. The Peruvian Delegate agreed with the suggestion from the Chair, but noted that this matter had already been clarified in Santiago upon a request from the then Ecuadorean delegate [El Señor Llosa manifiesta que está de acuerdo en que así se haga pero aclarando que esta conformidad ya quedó establecida en la Conferencia de Santiago como consta en el acta respectiva a pedido del Delegado de Ecuador señor González (the surname of the then

Ecuadorean delegate to the Santiago Conference was Fernández)].
Mr. Lara accepted the proposal from the Chair and his agreement is
recorded in the Minutes (Minutes 1954 First Session):

> The Delegate of Ecuador states that if the other countries con-
> sider that no explicit record is necessary, he agreed to record in
> the Minutes that the three countries deemed the matter on the
> dividing line of the jurisdictional waters settled and that said line
> was the parallel starting at the point at which the land boundary
> of the two countries reaches the sea. [El Señor delegado de Ecua-
> dor manifiesta que si los otros países consideran que no es necesa-
> rio una constancia expresa en el Convenio, él esta de acuerdo que
> conste en el Acta que los tres países consideran resuelto el punto
> de la línea divisoria de las aguas jurisdiccionales, que es el paralelo
> que parte del punto en que la frontera terrestre de ambos países
> llega al mar].

The following day, on 3 December 1954, after the Minutes of the previous day were circulated, Mr. Lara raised a point. He believed that the
Minutes merely recorded his views on the jurisdictional line, whereas
at the previous session the Chair had agreed to record that the three
countries were in agreement on this point:

> Following a reading of the Minutes, the Delegate of Ecuador,
> Mr. Salvador Lara, requested clarification of the statement made
> by the Chairman concerning the concept of the dividing line,
> since the Chairman had not proposed recording in the Minutes
> the statement made by the Delegate of Ecuador but that the three
> countries had agreed on the concept of the dividing line of the
> jurisdictional sea [Leída el Acta, el Señor Delegado del Ecua-
> dor, Salvador Lara, pidió que se aclarara lo manifestado por el
> señor Presidente respecto al concepto de la línea divisoria, pues el
> señor Presidente no había propuesto que quedara constancia en
> el Acta de las palabras del Delegado de Ecuador sino de que los
> tres países estaban de acuerdo en el concepto de línea divisoria
> del mar jurisdiccional].

The delegates from Chile and Peru accepted Mr. Lara's clarification
and approved the Minutes (Minutes 1954 Second Session).

Chile argued that the Minutes of the *Complementary Convention*
confirm that the *Santiago Declaration* delimited the entire lateral

boundary (CCM:141). Peru claimed that they merely confirm that Paragraph IV applied only to the maritime zones generated by islands (PR:191; *Compte Rendu* 2012/33:26 (Lowe)). Peru's argument is unconvincing because there was never any doubt that the text of Paragraph IV addressed the delimitation of the maritime zone of islands. Indeed, Mr. Lara's request can only be regarded as an attempt to preclude a strictly literal interpretation of Paragraph IV, which might lead to the conclusion that Paragraph IV only delimited the maritime zones of islands. Mr. Lara's request was unambiguous. He did not ask for a reinterpretation of Paragraph IV. He, along with the delegates from Chile and Peru, had no doubt that Paragraph IV applied to the entire lateral boundary. His objective was merely to insert a clause restating that, when the *Santiago Declaration* was approved, the understanding of the parties was that Paragraph IV applied to the entire lateral boundary. This is why in his request he stated that although the question of the 'dividing line of the jurisdictional sea' had been resolved in Santiago, he thought that it would not be 'redundant' to restate this point in the *Complementary Convention*. The Chilean and Peruvian delegates did not accede to his request because, in their view, Paragraph IV was 'very clear' (*bastante claro*). The exchange that followed prompted the parties to record in the Minutes that 'the three countries deemed the matter on the dividing line of the jurisdictional waters settled and that said line was the parallel starting at the point at which the land frontier between both two countries reaches the sea' [...los tres países consideran resuelto el punto de la linea divisoria de las aguas jurisdiccionales, que es el paralelo que parte del punto en que la frontera terrestre de ambos países llega al mar] (Minutes 1954 First Session). It is important to stress that Mr. Llosa, the Peruvian delegate agreed with this approach, but noted that this matter had been resolved in 1952 at the Conference in Santiago (Minutes 1954 First Session). The Minutes of the *Complementary Convention* thus provide unquestionable evidence that, in approving the text of Paragraph IV of the *Santiago Declaration,* the parties' understanding was that the parallel at the point where the land frontier reaches the sea was the lateral boundary—general and insular—of their respective claims.

3. Minutes of the Agreement Relating to a Special Maritime Frontier Zone

The Minutes of the *Agreement Relating to a Special Maritime Frontier Zone* (herafter *Special Agreement*) (Annex 3), provide further evidence that Paragraph IV delimited the general and the insular maritime zones of the three states. The objective of the *Special Agreement*, as its title suggests, was to establish a zone on both sides of the lateral boundary to tackle the problem of small vessels inadvertently crossing the boundary line, either because they lacked the equipment to determine the location of the boundary or because their crew had insufficient navigational knowledge to determine their position. The special zone created by the agreement (Article 1) extends 10 nm on either side of the boundary at a distance of 12 nm from the coast. The Agreement provides (Article 2) that the accidental presence of small vessels in the special zone will not be considered a violation of the waters of the maritime zone. It also notes that the establishment of the zone cannot be construed as creating rights deliberately to engage in hunting or fishing activities within the zone.

For the purpose of the interpretation of Paragraph IV of the *Santiago Declaration*, the key provision of this Agreement is Article 1:

> A special zone is hereby established, at a distance of 12 nautical miles from the coast, extending to a breadth of 10 nautical miles on either side of the parallel which constitutes the maritime boundary between the two countries.

The Minutes provide critical information about the wording of this Article. They read as follows: 'Upon the proposal by Mr. Salvador Lara, the concept already declared in Santiago that the parallel starting at the boundary point on the coast constitutes the maritime boundary between the neighbouring signatory countries, was incorporated into this article' [A propuesta del Señor Salvador Lara se incorporó en este artículo el concepto, ya declarado en Santiago, de que el paralelo que parte del punto limítrofe de la costa constituye el límite marítimo entre los países signatarios vecinos] (Minutes 1954 Second Session). The Minutes thus confirm that the phrase 'the parallel which constitutes the maritime boundary between the two countries', restates that the parties had delimited their entire lateral boundaries in 1952 at their Conference in Santiago.

Chile argued that Article 1 records the understanding of the three states that the lateral boundary between adjacent states follows a parallel of latitude (CCM:143). Peru attempted to minimize the importance of this Article, arguing that the reference to 'the maritime boundary between the two countries' meant that the Agreement was only applicable to Ecuador and Peru. The Court rejected this argument as it had no textual basis in the *Special Agreement* and because

Peru, in its own practice, had not interpreted it in such a restrictive manner (#85):

> In the view of the Court, there is nothing at all in the terms of the 1954 Special Maritime Frontier Zone Agreement which would limit it only to the Ecuador-Peru maritime boundary. Moreover Peru did not in practice accord it that limited meaning which would preclude its application to Peru's southern maritime boundary with Chile.

Peru also argued that the special zone established by the Agreement was unrelated to the boundary and that the use of the word 'parallel' in Article 1 had a purely practical meaning, without legal implications, since the parties had to find some way of identifying the special zone. The Court also rejected this argument. According to the Court, 'the terms of the 1954 Special Maritime Frontier Zone Agreement, especially Article 1 read with the preambular paragraphs, are clear. They acknowledge in a binding international agreement that a maritime boundary already exists' (#90). Yet, despite acknowledging that the parties had delimited their lateral maritime boundary by agreement, the Court refused to reconsider its interpretation of Paragraph IV of the *Santiago Declaration*. Instead, it concluded that the agreement mentioned in Article 1 of the *Special Agreement* was tacit.

The Court's conclusion that the reference to the maritime boundary refers to a tacit agreement is baffling since the Minutes of the Second Session of the 1954 Conference, held on 3 December, expressly note that the purpose of the changes to Article 1 was to restate a concept already agreed in Santiago in 1952. The Court, however, disregarded this important point, although in paragraph 73 of the Judgment it invokes the Minutes of the *Special Agreement* to explain that during the negotiations, the word 'parallel' was replaced by 'the parallel which constitutes the maritime boundary between the two countries'. This passage shows that while the Court consulted the Minutes of the *Special Agreement*, it failed to notice that they also explain the reason for the change.

4. *A note on the Minutes*

The Minutes of the *Santiago Declaration* and the Minutes of the two Lima Agreements show that the exchanges between the parties were made in good faith. Although the Minutes are not verbatim, they are neither imprecise nor self-serving. The parties naturally had conflicting views about the meaning and relevance of the Minutes, but did not challenge their accuracy. The preceding subsections show that, at several stages during the negotiations, the parties relied on the Minutes to clarify the meaning of provisions in the Agreements. In relation to Paragraph II of the *Declaration*, which defines the claim as extending to a minimum distance of 200 nm, the parties clarified in the Minutes that this provision was meant to enable the contracting parties unilaterally to extend the claim, but not to reduce it without the consent of the other two parties. Likewise, in the case of Paragraph VI of the Declaration, the parties clarified in the Minutes that the meaning of the phrase 'control and co-ordination' was a reference to products and resources of common interest. The parties' reliance on the Minutes to clarify the meaning of the terms they had agreed was so well established that even the Final Minutes of the Lima Conference contain two clarifications: one in relation to the *Special Agreement* and the other on a technical point to one of the agreements adopted at their First Conference in 1952. The clarification on the *Special Agreement* provides that the term 'accidental presence' of small vessels referred to in Article 2 was to be determined exclusively by the authorities of the country whose maritime jurisdictional boundary had been transgressed (*Final Minutes of the Second Conference on Conservation and Exploitation of the Marine Resources of the South Pacific*, CCM: Annex No. 40).

Paragraph IV of the *Declaration* was a focus of interest for the parties during their Conferences in 1952 and 1954. The Minutes of these Conferences provide a comprehensive account of the negotiating process on points relevant to its interpretation. The Minutes of the *Santiago Declaration* show that when the parties agreed to amend the text of the Draft Agreement, their intention was to delimit the entire lateral boundary. While the 1952 Minutes do not provide sufficient evidence to establish that the parties had indeed delimited their lateral boundary, the Minutes of the *Complementary Convention* clarify this point. They explain why the parties decided not to include any reference to the lateral boundary and provide a detailed record of how this decision was taken. In particular, they record the parties' understanding that the *Santiago Declaration* had delimited the entire lateral boundary. Likewise, the Minutes of the *Special Agreement*, confirm that the phrase in Article 1 of the Agreement, which refers to 'the parallel which constitutes the maritime boundary between the two countries', was restating a concept already agreed in Santiago and reflected in Paragraph IV of the Declaration. The Minutes therefore provide critically important information on the ordinary meaning of Paragraph IV. It is incredible that the Court disregarded them without offering any explanation. In this connection, it is helpful to recall Sir Hersh Lauterpacht's advice that

> it is the duty of the Judge…to refrain from neglecting any possible clues, however troublesome may be their examination and however liable they may be to abuse, which may reveal or render clear the intention of the authors of the rule to be interpreted.
>
> (Lauterpacht 1949:83; see also, Fitzmaurice 1957:207)

In this case, since the Minutes of the *Complementary Convention* and the *Special Agreement* provide critical information for the interpretation of Paragraph IV, it is unreasonable to disregard them. These Minutes are not a supplementary means of interpretation, but an integral part of their respective Agreements (YILC 1964 (II):57–58). This interpretation is consistent with Sir Eric Beckett's concept of a treaty. Sir Eric, well-known for his scepticism about excessive reliance on preparatory work, conceded that, for the purpose of interpretation, Minutes should, in some cases, be regarded as part of the treaty. In his view, the

> treaty will, of course, include everything that was signed at the time even though this consists of a main document, called the treaty, together with a whole lot of letters, protocols and even (probably) agreed minutes. Further, the treaty for this purpose may include something more still. In addition to everything which is published and registered, there may exist yet further specially initialled minutes which have deliberately been prepared for the purpose of its interpretation.
>
> (Beckett 1950:442; see also Fitzmaurice 1951:12)

The Minutes of the *Complementary Convention*, which accurately and precisely record the parties' views on the meaning of Paragraph IV, and the Minutes of the *Special Agreement*, which unequivocally refer to the boundary as reflected in the agreement concluded in Santiago in 1952, fall squarely within Sir Eric's conception of what should be considered to be part of the treaty. (See also Dissenting Opinion of Judges Basdevant, Winiarski, McNair and Read in *Conditions of Admission of a State to Membership in the United Nations (Article 4 of the Charter)* (Advisory Opinion), I.C.J. Reports 1948, 57 at 82).

E. The 1968–1969 Lighthouse Arrangements

As noted in Section B(4), above, the analysis of the 1968/69 Lighthouse Arrangements was the Court's only explicit attempt to test whether its interpretation of Paragraph IV was sound. The Arrangements were designed to ensure compliance with the maritime boundary agreed in 1952. During the years leading up to this process, Chile and Peru exchanged several diplomatic notes in which they expressed concern about repeated violations of their respective territorial waters (PM: Annexes 67–69). These documents make it clear that both parties understood that it was their duty to complain about alleged violations of their boundary. To this effect, they agreed to install 'leading marks visible from the sea to materialise the parallel of the maritime frontier originating at Boundary Marker number one (*No. 1*)' (#96). It was thus that they built two lighthouses, on either side of their land boundary, near boundary marker (*Hito*) No. 1.

Chile argued that the exchanges leading to the erection of the lighthouses confirm the parties' understanding that a maritime frontier was already in place. Peru, on the other hand, highlighting the fact that the parties did not make reference to a delimitation agreement in their exchanges, argued that the decision to build the lighthouses was not intended to establish a permanent maritime boundary. It was merely a practical measure designed to separate Chilean and Peruvian fishing vessels within a limited range of 15 nm from the coast.

The Court's view on the Lighthouse Agreements was as follow (#99):

> The Court is of the opinion that the purpose and geographical scope of the arrangements were limited, as indeed the Parties recognize. The Court also observes that the record of the process leading to the arrangements and the building of the lighthouses does not refer to any pre-existent delimitation agreement. What is important in the Court's view, however, is that the arrangements proceed on the basis that a maritime boundary extending along the parallel beyond 12 nautical miles already exists. Along with the 1954 Special Maritime Frontier Zone Agreement, the arrangements acknowledge that fact. Also, like that Agreement, they do not indicate the extent and nature of that maritime boundary. The arrangements seek to give effect to it for a specific purpose.

The Court correctly notes that the correspondence relating to the Lighthouse Arrangements does not mention a pre-existent delimitation agreement. Yet, although the correspondence on the Lighthouse Arrangements confirms that there was a common boundary along the parallel of latitude, the Court does not find that this evidence contradicts its finding that Paragraph IV had not delimited the parties' lateral boundary. Instead, the Court relies on this evidence to strengthen its conclusion that the parties had entered into a tacit agreement.

According to the Court, the Lighthouse Arrangements complement and confirm its interpretation of Article 1 of the *Special Agreement*, which had led it to conclude that the parties had entered into a tacit agreement. In both instances it interprets the reference to a maritime boundary as a reference to a boundary delimited by tacit agreement. When the Court interpreted Article 1 of the *Special Agreement* it did not contemplate that it might contradict its interpretation of Paragraph IV of the *Declaration*. Likewise, in its interpretation of the Lighthouse Arrangements, the Court did not consider that it could possibly contradict its interpretation of Paragraph IV of the *Declaration*. It uses these exchanges to reinforce its finding on the tacit agreement, rather than as a challenge to its interpretation of Paragraph IV. Thus, the Court's role shifts from that of umpire adjudicating the parties' claims to advocate, determined to justify its finding that the parties had entered into a tacit agreement. The Court's reluctance to reconsider its interpretation of Paragraph IV of the *Declaration* is disappointing. It is also unconvincing because it assumes that seventeen years after the 1952 *Declaration*, the parties were busy 'materialising' the first 15 miles of their boundary along the parallel, but had no interest in formalising a tacit agreement which, according to the Court, had been concluded before 1954. This assumption calls into question not only the Court's narrow interpretation of Paragraph IV, but also its finding on the tacit agreement.

F. Ordinary meaning and context

The Court's finding that Paragraph IV of the *Declaration* delimited only a small segment of the parties' lateral boundary would be plausible if the focus is exclusively on the text, not its context or its object and purpose. Given the effort and care shown by the CEP countries to establish a comprehensive legal framework to define, protect and govern every aspect relating to their maritime claim, the notion that they did not delimit their general lateral boundary is not credible. In the language of the VCLT, such a finding is absurd and cannot be reconciled with the carefully crafted regulatory framework reflected in the ten agreements concluded by the CEP countries between 1952 and 1954. Given this detailed framework, it is unreasonable to assume that the parties did not define the lateral boundaries of their respective maritime claims. On this point, it is interesting to recall that, when the Court rejected Chile's argument that the second sentence of Paragraph IV presupposed the delimitation of the entire boundary, it noted that the parties' narrow concern with the maritime boundary of islands was justified because 'it appeared that the State parties intended to resolve a specific issue which could obviously create possible future tension between them by agreeing that the parallel would delimit insular zones' (#61). Paradoxically, however, the Court's acknowledgement of the parties' foresight in resolving future problems in connection with islands, does not question its own finding that the parties were not interested in resolving the more important question concerning their general lateral boundaries. The incongruity that results from the Court's narrow interpretation disappears when, as prescribed by Article 31(1) of the VCLT, Paragraph IV is interpreted in its context and in the light of its object and purpose. Such approach would lead to the conclusion that this paragraph delimited the entire lateral boundary.

The Minutes of the *Complementary Convention* and of the *Special Agreement* confirm that the parties adopted Paragraph IV on the understanding they were delimiting the entire lateral boundary. This was the sense that they attached to Paragraph IV and is, therefore, its ordinary meaning in accordance with Article 31(1) of the VCLT. This interpretation is consistent with fundamental principles underlying the rules of treaty interpretation of the VCLT: that the terms of the treaty reflect the intention of the parties; and, that the meaning of the terms of a treaty are determined by their context. In this case, the Minutes of the *Complementary Convention* and the Minutes of the *Special Agreement* provide evidence that the parties were in no doubt that Paragraph IV had delimited their entire lateral boundary, when they concluded the *Santiago Declaration*. If the objective of interpretation is to determine the intention of the parties, as reflected in the text of the treaty, it is essential to take into account evidence of the sense in which the parties employed the terms in the treaty. Stanley Fish, who believes that there can be no meaning without identifying the parties' intentions, argues that 'theoretically, nothing stands in the way of any string of words becoming the vehicle of any intention' (Fish 2005:634). His views reflect a well-established approach to legal interpretation. Indeed, according to Philip Jessup—a prominent international lawyer and former judge of the ICJ—'the function of interpretation is to ascertain the design of the parties, always bearing in mind that they are free to employ the words in any sense they choose' (Jessup 1947:391).

In this passage Jessup is restating, as well as endorsing, the views of Professor Charles Hyde, who in 1909, argued as follows (Hyde 1909:48):

> Whatever be its form, evidence of the signification attached by the parties to the terms of their compact should not be excluded from the consideration of a tribunal entrusted with the duty of interpretation. When the fact is established that the parties adopted a particular standard of interpretation—that they used expressions with a particular signification of their own choice—it is immaterial how widely that signification may differ from any other.

The Court's failure to examine the context of Paragraph IV is probably explained by the irresistible appeal of the strictly textual approach to interpretation combined with reluctance to consider any document that might be regarded as extraneous to the text of the treaty. This perspective is odd, because, as Sir Humphrey Waldock stated, contextual elements—in particular Article 31(2)(a) of the VCLT—are not a supplementary or extraneous means of interpretation (YILC 1964 (II): 57–58). Despite this authoritative view several commentators continue to regard the context as little more than a supplementary means of interpretation. Richard Gardiner, for example, draws a sharp distinction between ordinary meaning and context. He regards the context as independent of the ordinary meaning of the terms of the treaty. In his view, 'the primary reason for looking to the context is to confirm an ordinary meaning' (Gardiner 2008:178; see also, Linderfalk 2007:102; but see, Dorr 2012:549–550; Villiger 2009:427).

The prevalence of the strictly textual approach to treaty interpretation also explains why Chile, while invoking the Minutes of the *Santiago Declaration* and of the Lima Conventions, did not claim them to be essential components for determining the ordinary meaning of Paragraph IV. Instead it characterised them as evidence of the parties' agreement on the interpretation of Paragraph IV. Its reluctance to argue that they were context for the interpretation of the *Declaration* is not altogether surprising. Indeed, in its written pleadings, Chile offers a superficial interpretation of the standard clause in the Lima Agreements, which provided that these agreements were integral and supplementary to the agreements concluded in Santiago in 1952 (Section B3(b), above). It describes the standard clause, condescendingly and erroneously, as a clause employed mainly in civil law countries:

> The States parties' use of this technique is not surprising given that all of them had civil-law traditions, in which a later instrument

(such as a law or agreement) can supplement or authentically interpret an earlier instrument, such that the two must be read together.
(CR:94)

Reluctance to follow Sir Humphrey Waldock's authoritative advice on the nature and importance of context is also evident in the Opinions of the judges who disagreed with the Court's interpretation of Paragraph IV. In their Joint Dissenting Opinion, Judges Xue, Gaja, Bhandari and ad hoc Judge Orrego Vicuña accepted Chile's argument that Paragraph IV had implicitly delimited the maritime zones generated by continental coasts' (Joint Dissent #7). Although they acknowledged that the 1954 Minutes of the *Complementary Convention* gave 'some support' to their interpretation, they regarded them as a supplementary means of interpretation, not as part of the context. Even President Tomka, who strongly disagreed with the Court's interpretation, was unable to distance himself from the strictly textual approach. In his view, it would be 'a step too far to assert that the 1952 Declaration expressly established the parallel as the boundary between the zones of Chile and Peru, respectively' (Tomka #13). Nevertheless, relying on the Minutes of the *Complementary Convention* and the *Special Agreement* he argued that at the Lima Conference the parties agreed 'to confirm that their 1952 Santiago Declaration was adopted on the understanding that the parallel starting at the point where their land frontier reaches the sea constituted the line dividing the zones they respectively claimed' (Tomka #16). He concluded, however, that 'the Santiago Declaration should serve as evidence of the Parties' recognition of a settlement, and not as the actual legal source of that settlement' (Tomka #22). Thus, although he arrives at this conclusion, his Separate Opinion shows that, in his view, the ordinary meaning of Paragraph IV is independent of its context.

G. Final remarks

The Court's reluctance to respond to some of the arguments made by the parties, especially in connection with the Minutes of the Lima Agreements, raises questions about the performance of its judicial function. Obviously, courts are not obliged to respond to all the arguments presented, but they should not ignore important arguments. As Sir Robert Jennings noted,

> hearing a party includes taking due account of what it says....This is not to suggest that all arguments must be dealt with seriatim in

the judgment. It is, however, to suggest that a court that appears to have approached the hearing of a case with its mind already made up, and to have listened to the parties only in order to conform to the requirements of procedural rules, or courtesy or habit, wholly fails to act as a court of law.

(Jennings 1997:43)

Judges Bedjaoui, Ranjeva and Koroma made a similar point in their Joint Dissenting Opinion in *Maritime Delimitation and Territorial Questions between Qatar and Bahrain,* Merits. In their view, when the Court does not respond to numerous legal grounds argued by the parties it gives 'the regrettable impression that it has only given the Parties a very incomplete hearing on matters which they however considered to be crucial' (I.C.J. Reports 2001, 40 at 145).

Part II
The tacit agreement

As explained in Part I, the Court found that although the parties had not delimited their lateral boundary by express agreement, they had done so tacitly. This finding was based on an inference drawn from a provision in the *Special Agreement* of 1954, which indicates that there was a maritime boundary running along the parallel. This finding, neither anticipated nor desired by the parties, gave the Court enormous discretion to design a tacit agreement, without taking into account the comprehensive legal framework established by the parties to regulate their maritime claim. The parties were not given the opportunity to address any question relating to the tacit agreement, which had the effect of reinforcing the Court's power.

Part II discusses the three main issues arising from the problematic finding on the tacit agreement: the reasoning and evidence that led the Court to conclude that the parties had entered into tacit agreement; the way the Court determined the content of the agreement; and the role played by international law in shaping the tacit agreement. The final remarks ask whether more adequate evidence would have enabled the Court to make a stronger case for the tacit agreement and whether its supposedly equitable outcome was the result of combining the rules on treaty interpretation with the rules on maritime delimitation.

A. Reasoning and evidence

1. Inference versus legal interpretation

The Court did not find it easy to explain how and when the parties had entered into a tacit agreement. Indeed, one of the few points on which the parties agreed was that their boundary had not been delimited by tacit agreement. Peru rejected this possibility because its main argument was that no agreement had defined the parties' lateral boundaries

(PM:13; see also *Compte Rendu* 2012/29:24–25 (Lowe); *Compte Rendu* 2012/33:14 (Lowe)). Chile discarded it because its central argument was that Paragraph IV of the *Santiago Declaration* had delimited the parties' lateral boundary (*Compte Rendu* 2012/30:74 (Crawford); *Compte Rendu* 2012/36:37 (Crawford); *Compte Rendu* 2012/31:41 (Petrochilos)). Thus, the Court could not rely on the parties' arguments to justify its finding on the tacit agreement. This explains why, at times, this section of the Judgment reads more like a partisan brief than a decision by a court of law.

The Court's finding that the parties had concluded a tacit agreement was based upon Article 1 of the *Special Agreement* (Annex 3). It reads as follow:

> A special zone is hereby established, at a distance of 12 nautical miles from the coast, extending to a breadth of 10 nautical miles on either side of the parallel which constitutes the maritime boundary between the two countries.

This Article established an exemption for the benefit of small vessels. Under the exemption, small vessels were not penalized if they accidentally crossed the maritime boundary, either because they lacked adequate navigational instruments or because their crew was unable to determine their position at sea. The exemption applied only within a special zone established by the Agreement and did not create the right deliberately to engage in hunting or fishing within the zone.

Judge Sepúlveda-Amor, in his Declaration, described the finding that the parties had concluded a tacit agreement as an unwarranted legal inference (Sepúlveda-Amor #11). Legal inferences, according to Sir Gerald Fitzmaurice, can be drawn only after the meaning of the relevant legal provision is firmly established. In his view, relying on the 'inferential process in order to establish the meaning is…to put the cart before the horse…' (Fitzmaurice 1963:154). The Court should have tried to establish the meaning of the phrase 'maritime boundary' in Article 1 of the *Special Agreement,* before deciding that the parties had entered into a tacit agreement. Instead, it hastily concluded that the phrase 'maritime boundary' was a reference to a tacit agreement This inference is questionable because, as noted in Part I, the Minutes of the *Special Agreement* clearly show that the phrase 'the parallel constituting the maritime boundary' was introduced into the Agreement at the request of the delegate from Ecuador, in order to reaffirm a point already resolved by the *Santiago Declaration*. The Minutes of the *Complementary Convention*, also concluded in Lima, reinforce the point that the *Santiago Declaration* had delimited the lateral boundary. The Court, however, ignoring this evidence, inferred that the parties had concluded a tacit agreement. This finding is, thus, a textbook example of an inference that puts the cart before the horse.

The Court's inference also created an artificial dilemma. Article 1 of the *Special Agreement* provides that the lateral boundary of the special zone extends 12 (nm) from the coast along the parallel, but does not expressly indicate its seaward extension (#92). This omission provided the Court with the opportunity to determine the extent of the lateral boundary. The Minutes of the *Special Agreement* reveal, however, that the *Special Agreement* does not mention its extent because this had been settled in 1952. The Court's interpretation of Article 1 is also implausible because it assumes that, while in the *Special Agreement* the parties established a special zone running along both sides of the maritime boundary, they carelessly forgot to indicate the boundary's entire seaward extension. A careful examination of the *Special Agreement* shows, however, that Article 2 implicitly refers to the extension of the lateral boundary. Article 2 provides that vessels benefiting from the exemption include those involved in fishing and hunting activities. It reads as follow:

> The accidental presence in the said zone [the special zone] of a vessel of either of the adjacent countries, which is a vessel of the nature described in the paragraph beginning with the words 'Experience has shown' in the preamble hereto [small vessels], shall not be considered to be a violation of the waters of the maritime zone, though this provision shall not be construed as recognizing any right to engage, with deliberate intent, in hunting or fishing in the said special zone.

The reference to hunting confirms that whale hunting was one of the activities to be placed in the special zone. The reference to hunting was not accidental: the Minutes of the Conference show that the intention of the parties was that the special exemption should benefit both fishing and hunting activities carried out by small vessels. Their intention is reflected in the title of the draft agreement: *Convention for the Establishment of a Neutral Zone for Fishing and Hunting in the Maritime Frontier of the Neighbouring Countries* (*Convenio sobre el Establecimiento de Zona Neutra de Pesca y Caza en la Frontera Marina de los Países Vecinos*). This title was abandoned when the delegate from Ecuador requested during the negotiations that the word 'neutral' be removed from the title. Thus, the title of the agreement was changed to *Special Maritime Frontier Zone Agreement.* The removal of fishing and hunting from the title did not, however, entail a shift in the parties' intention to include these two activities. Although in paragraph 73 the Court noted that the phrase 'neutral zone' in the title was replaced by 'special maritime frontier zone', it failed to notice that the original title included hunting and that the reference to hunting was not removed from the text of the agreement. Since Article 2 confirms that whale hunting was one of the activities covered by the *Special Agreement,* and there is substantial evidence that this activity was carried out within the entire 200 nm area, it is odd that the Court did not infer that the seaward extension of the special zone was also 200 nm; that is, the same as the parties' maritime claim (more on this point below).

President Tomka, who also considered that the special zone extended to the whole length of the parties' maritime claim, approached this question from a different angle. In his Declaration, he pointed out that the parties' silence regarding the extent of the lateral boundary

> can only lead to the conclusion that the special maritime zone was meant to extend seaward along the parallel up until the limit of the Parties' maritime entitlements, for a distance which also corresponded to their claimed maritime zones at that time.
>
> (Tomka #3)

The four dissenting judges—Judges Xue, Gaja, Bhandari and ad hoc Judge Orrego Vicuña—agreeing with President Tomka, noted that the reference to the parallel in Article 1 was a reference to the parallel identified in the *Santiago Declaration* (Joint Dissent #22). Moreover, recalling the contextual coherence between the Lima and Santiago Conferences, the four dissenting judges argued that the interpretation of the *Special Agreement* could not possibly lead 'to the conclusion that Peru and Chile had tacitly agreed on a maritime boundary that is much shorter than that agreed among the parties to the Santiago Declaration' (Joint Dissent #23).

The view that the seaward extent of the special zone was 200 nm was also shared by Peru. Although Peru argued that the phrase 'maritime boundary' in the *Special Agreement* described a functional fisheries line, not a boundary, it admitted that it was established in an area of the high seas within which the parties claimed functional jurisdiction (PM:98, 143). Peru also carefully distinguished the special zone established by the *Special Agreement* from the area covered by the Lighthouse Arrangements of 1968–1969. While the objective of the Lighthouse Arrangements was to avoid friction between the parties within 12 nm from the coast, the zone established by the *Special Agreement* started 12 nm from the coast (PM:151).

It should also be noted that only one of the six agreements concluded in Lima explicitly mentions the 200 nm claim. The exception is the *Complementary Convention* (Annex 2), which reaffirms the parties' commitment to defending the 200 nm claim. The other five Agreements, which deal with different regulatory aspects within the zones claimed by the parties, do not mention the seaward extent. This suggests that the parties were careful to ensure that each of the six Agreements concluded at the Lima Conference focused strictly on their respective subject matter. This is why, in the *Complementary Convention*, Chile and Peru did not accede to the Ecuadorian delegate's request to restate that the lateral boundary was the parallel, because this matter had been decided at the Conference in Santiago. Since the other five Agreements concluded in Lima in 1954 are connected to the *Complementary Convention* and, by virtue of the standard clause, are also connected to the four Agreements concluded in Santiago in 1952, there can be little doubt that they concerned regulatory aspects within well-defined maritime zones having a seaward extension of 200 nm.

2. Agreement or evolving understanding?

Tacit consent plays an important role in international law, particularly in connection with the acceptance of reservations and amendments to multilateral treaties (Aust 2000:113, 115, 180; Brunnée 2012:352, 356; Churchill and Ulfstein 2000; Fitzmaurice 2005, 1997; Villiger 2009:103, 177, 209–210, 220, 285, 289–293; Widdows 1976:120). In general, however, the consent of states to international obligations is expressed in writing and often surrounded by strict formalities, including signature, exchange of instruments and ratification. While formal procedures are largely designed to ensure that international legal obligations are not lightly presumed, international law accepts that states can express their consent by other means. Thus, although the Vienna Convention on the Law of Treaties applies to agreements in written form (Article 2), it acknowledges (Article 3) that the rules of the Convention may also apply to agreements not in written form (see also YILC 1966 (II):190).

In any event, agreements, whether tacit or explicit, must be based upon an accord or meeting of the minds between the parties. In the case of tacit agreements, the parties' intention to enter into an agreement is inferred from their conduct. As the Court noted in a previous case, which it recalls in paragraph 91 of the Judgment, 'evidence of a tacit legal agreement must be compelling' *Territorial and Maritime Dispute between Nicaragua and Honduras in the Caribbean Sea (Nicaragua v. Honduras)*, Judgment, I.C.J Reports 2007, 659, paragraph 253, at 735). In that case, the Court rejected the claim that oil concessions granted by the parties justified the conclusion that they had tacitly established a maritime boundary (Ibid., paragraph 254). A year later, in *Pedra Branca*, the Court acknowledged that a tacit agreement might bring about the transfer of sovereignty, but was careful to note that 'any passing of sovereignty over territory on the basis of the conduct of the Parties...must be manifested clearly and without any doubt by that conduct and the relevant facts' (*Sovereignty over Pedra Branca/Pulau Batu Puteh, Middle Rocks and South Ledge (Malaysia/Singapore)*, Judgment, I.C.J. Reports 2008, 12 at 51). In the light of these authoritative statements, it is necessary to ask whether, in this case, the evidence of the tacit agreement was compelling and whether the parties, by their conduct, manifested their accord clearly and without doubt.

In paragraph 91 the Court observes that:

> [I]n this case, the Court has before it an Agreement [the *Special Agreement*] which makes clear that the maritime boundary along a parallel already existed between the Parties. The 1954 Agreement is decisive in this respect. That Agreement cements the tacit agreement.
> (#91)

This finding, however, is not supported by evidence of any act, or omission, indicating that the parties had concluded a tacit agreement. In the absence of such evidence, it is not clear how the *Special Agreement* could have performed the supposed cementing function. As Judge Sebutinde notes in her Dissenting Opinion, the Court does not provide evidence that there was 'a meeting of the minds between the Parties' and hence failed to demonstrate that the parties had entered into a tacit agreement (Sebutinde #3). The Court's failure to provide evidence created confusion about the date of the agreement. Judge Sepúlveda-Amor, who in his Declaration argues that the Court failed to trace the origins of the tacit agreement, asks what happened between 1952 and 1954 that might justify the conclusion that the parties entered into a tacit agreement (Sepúlveda-Amor #8). In his Separate Opinion Judge Owada expresses a similar concern (Owada #17). Since the Court found that the *Santiago Declaration* had not delimited the lateral boundary, it might seem reasonable to assume that the tacit agreement was concluded sometime between the end of the Santiago Conference (August 1952) and the start of the Lima Conference (December 1954). The Court, however, does not provide any indication about the likely date of the agreement. Judge Skotnikov's Declaration reflects the confusion. Although he agrees that the parties concluded a tacit agreement, he suggests it was concluded before the *Santiago Declaration*, sometime between 1947 and 1952 (Skotnikov #2). Judge Skotnikov's view on the possible date of the agreement coincides with the view of Chile's Acting Legal Adviser who, in an Internal Memo of 1964, argued that the agreement delimiting the lateral boundary was concluded before the Santiago Conference of 1952. This Memo, however, as the Court acknowledged, does not suggest that the agreement was tacit (#93).

The confusion over the date of the tacit agreement explains why the Court opted to use the language employed in *Pedra Branca*. It argued that there had been an 'evolving understanding between the parties concerning their maritime boundary' (#91). It finds evidence of this 'evolving understanding' in two observations made earlier in the Judgment: one in connection with the interpretation of the parties' Unilateral Proclamations of 1947 (#43); and the other in connection with the interpretation of the 1952 *Santiago Declaration* (#69). Neither of these observations is particularly helpful. In paragraph 43 of the Judgment the Court observes that the Unilateral Proclamations of 1947 do not reflect a shared understanding concerning maritime delimitation, but notes, nonetheless, that they contain similar claims 'giving rise to the necessity of establishing lateral limits of the zones in the future'. Since this observation unequivocally rules out the possibility that, at the time, the parties had a shared understanding concerning their maritime boundaries, it is difficult to see how it can be invoked as evidence of such understanding. The second observation follows immediately after the Court concluded, in paragraph 68, that there was nothing in the *travaux préparatoires* that contradicted its view that the *Santiago Declaration* had not delimited the entire maritime boundary. The observation in paragraph 69 reads as follow:

> Nevertheless, various factors mentioned in the preceding paragraphs, such as the original Chilean proposal and the use of the parallel as the limit of the maritime zone of an island of one State party located less than 200 nautical miles from the general maritime zone of another State party, suggest that there might have been some sort of shared understanding among the States parties of a more general nature concerning their maritime boundaries. The Court will return to this matter later.

It is difficult to ascertain what the Court means when it states 'there might have been some sort of shared understanding among the States parties of a more general nature concerning their maritime boundaries'. Given that, in the preceding paragraph, the Court had clearly stated that the *Santiago Declaration* had not delimited the entire lateral boundary, its conjecture about the parties' state of mind is implausible, as it assumes that, despite sharing a common view about the location of the lateral boundary, they decided, nonetheless, not to make it explicit. In paragraph 91, the Court returns to this point—as promised in paragraph 69. Yet, paragraph 91 refers the reader back to paragraphs 43 and 69. This cross-reference does not throw any light on the supposed shared understanding or on the date of the tacit agreement. It simply begs the question and leads to the introduction of a questionable distinction between the form and content of the tacit agreement. The Court derives the form of the tacit agreement from an inference based on a hurried misreading of Article 1 of the *Special Agreement*. Since the Court does not provide any evidence about how the parties established the tacit agreement, the agreement has no content. It is an empty shell. The Court, therefore, filled it with content by examining the practice of the parties in the early and mid-1950s (#103). After separating the form of the agreement from its content, the Court dropped any further reference to the parties' shared understanding.

Judge Sepúlveda-Amor strongly criticized the form and content distinction proposed by the Court. In his view, the form of a tacit agreement cannot be seen as independent or separate from its substance (Sepúlveda-Amor #16). Judge Owada agreed and offered an alternative approach. In his view, the Court's interpretation 'rests on factually quite dubious grounds' because Article 1 of the 1954 Agreement does not support the Court's inference about the tacit agreement (Owada #14). Instead, he argued that the parties had engaged in a long-standing practice, which he describes as a de facto delimitation (Owada #26(2)), which, at some stage 'crystallized into a normative rule that the Parties came to recognize as constituting the legal delimitation of their respective zones of maritime entitlement' (Owada #26(3)). He did not precisely specify the date when this practice became normative, but noted, however, that it was sometime between the 1950s and 1970s. According to Judge Owada the role of the *Special Agreement* was merely to consolidate the legal title based on tacit acceptance through practice (Owada #26(6)).

Judge Owada's proposal is, undoubtedly, a serious attempt to introduce some coherence to the Court's finding about the tacit agreement. He does not, however, explain how the *Special Agreement* contributed to consolidating the legal title of a practice that, in his view, began in 1950 and lasted until 1970. His Opinion is also unpersuasive, based as it is on the erroneous assumptions that between the 1950s and 1970s the only activity occurring along the boundary involved artisanal fishing carried out within 50 nm from the shore (more on this below). The Court did not endorse Judge Owada's approach, choosing instead to pursue the distinction between the form and content of the agreement: its form, an empty shell derived from a problematic legal inference; and its content, derived by the Court from its interpretation of the practice of the parties.

B. Content of the Agreement

Article 1 of the 1954 *Special Maritime Frontier Zone Agreement* contains basic, but limited information about the lateral boundary. It confirms that the lateral boundary runs along 'the parallel which constitutes the maritime boundary between the two states' and that the special zone established by that agreement starts a distance of 12 nm from the coast. Thus, it fell upon the Court to determine the nature and the extent of the boundary.

1. Nature of the boundary

The question concerning the nature of the boundary involved deciding whether the tacit agreement had delimited only the parties' territorial sea—described by the Court as the water column—or whether it included all the areas claimed by the parties in the *Declaration*, including the 200 nm maritime zone.

The parties indirectly addressed the question about the nature of the boundary within the context of their respective arguments. Chile argued that the boundary was an all-purpose boundary. According to Chile, in the *Santiago Declaration* the parties 'claimed plenitude of sovereignty and jurisdiction, and delimited that claim *inter se*, ... [establishing] an all-purpose maritime boundary' (CCM:294–295). Peru, rejecting the view that the *Declaration* had delimited the boundary, argued that the word 'boundary', as used in the *Special Agreement* of 1954, was merely a functional line aimed at policing fisheries and facilitating shipping (PM:95). Peru also argued that the parties could not have agreed to an all-purpose boundary since, at the time, international law did not recognise the existence of any maritime zone other than the territorial sea (PM:98).

The Court found that the tacitly agreed boundary was an all-purpose boundary (#102):

> The tacit agreement, acknowledged in the 1954 Agreement, must be understood in the context of the 1947 Proclamations and the

1952 Santiago Declaration. These instruments expressed claims to
the sea-bed and to waters above the sea-bed and their resources.
In this regard the Parties drew no distinction, at that time or sub-
sequently, between these spaces. The Court concludes that the
boundary is an all-purpose one.

This finding is surprising because it is based on an inference drawn
from three instruments which, according to the Court, had not delimited the parties' lateral boundary (#43 and ##60–61). The Court does
not explain how these instruments could have determined the nature
of the boundary, but not delimited it. This finding is also puzzling because paragraph 102 (above) refers to the parties' claim to the seabed,
the waters above the seabed and their resources, but does not mention
the parties' 200 nm claim. This is a strange omission because the 200
nm claim is the most distinctive feature of these three instruments.
Judge Owada highlighted the flaw in the Court's reasoning:

> If the Parties, for whatever reason and under whatever circum-
> stances, had come to accept the parallel of latitude as the definitive
> maritime boundary line for all purposes, as the Judgment assumes it
> to be... then there should be no reason to think that this line should
> terminate at a distance of 80 nautical miles from the starting-point.
> It could instead extend to the maximum of 200 nautical miles.
>
> (Owada #12)

According to Judge Owada, if the line were to stop at any point less
than 200 nm, it would not be an all-purpose boundary. It would simply
be a de facto line, a functional line that could not be the product of
a tacit agreement. The contradiction noted by Judge Owada did not
trouble the Court, because the odd reasoning underlying the finding
on the nature of the boundary was an important step in a chain of
reasoning that enabled the Court to determine the extent of the lateral
boundary without taking into account the 200 nm claim.

2. *Extent of the lateral boundary*

The terms of reference set by the Court for its inquiry into the extent
of the maritime boundary involved an investigation into the practice of
the parties in the early and mid-1950s and an examination of contextual
elements, including 'developments in the law of the sea at that time'
(#103). Despite its broad terms of reference, its findings are disappointing. As noted in Part I, Section B(4), the Court did not find any evidence

to help determine the extent of the lateral boundary, even though it devoted considerable space to the analysis of the practice of the parties (##119–142). As a consequence, the only evidence on which it could base its finding was on the incomplete information provided by the parties on their fishing activities. The Court's main conclusion from this inquiry is that 'the principal maritime activity in the early 1950s was fishing undertaken by small vessels' (#109) and, that, as a consequence, the extent of the lateral boundary is merely 80 nm (##117, 149 and 151).

This finding is unconvincing on several grounds: (1) it does not take whale hunting into account, one of the parties' major maritime activities at the time; (2) it relies on scant and inadequate information on the parties' fishing activities; (3) it does not take into account that the parties' fishing activities underwent important changes during the relevant period; and (4) it does not provide any information about the size of the vessels, even though its finding is based on the assertion that only small vessels operated in the area.

The Court's inquiry into the practice of the parties assumes, incorrectly, that the 200 nm claim was not a relevant factor. This assumption enabled the Court to focus exclusively on fishing activities while disregarding whale hunting, which took place well beyond the 80 nm limit set by the Court (Loring 1971:399). In order to disregard the 200 nm claim the Court relied on a series of questionable interpretative twists to depict it as a mere political demand, designed to attract international solidarity and to keep distant fishing fleets away from the region. In paragraph 109 the Court observed that the *Special Agreement* of 1954 revealed that the parties were only concerned with the activities of the local population. It then added—suggesting that this concern was overriding—that 'it does not see as of great significance their knowledge of the likely or possible extent of the resources out to 200 nautical miles nor the extent of their fishing in later years'. The reason the Court concluded that the resources outside the immediate area of the coast were not significant was because it assumed that the parties' fishing activities at the time were undertaken by small vessels. Yet, since in paragraph 102 the Court had found that the boundary was an all-purpose boundary, the Court had to add a caveat noting that, in itself, the evidence concerning fisheries, 'cannot be determinative of the extent of that boundary' (#111). This caveat, however, is immediately reversed by a statement discarding the importance of the 200 nm claim:

> Nevertheless, the fisheries activity provides some support for the view that the Parties, at the time when they acknowledged the

existence of an agreed maritime boundary between them, were unlikely to have considered that it extended all the way to the 200-nautical-mile limit.

(#111)

Since the Court did not find any other relevant evidence, it concluded that the primary concern of the parties 'regarding the more distant waters…was with presenting a position of solidarity, in particular, in respect of the major third countries involved in long distance fisheries' (#150). It then added that, because the parties were concerned with generating solidarity, with respect to the exclusion of long distance fisheries, they did not provide precise information as on the extent of the boundary (#150). Thus, according to the Court, the parties' efforts to seek international solidarity in support of the 200 nm claim led them to overlook the question of the extent of the lateral boundary. This view is implausible. What is clear, however, is that, through a series of speculative and contradictory observations, the Court makes the 200 nm claim disappear, thus clearing the way to focus exclusively on the parties' fishing activities. Nevertheless, the Court does not seem entirely at ease with this approach. Indeed, in paragraph 151, the Court chastises the parties for entering into a tacit agreement that provides so little information about the extent of the boundary:

> The material before the Court concerning the Parties' focus on solidarity in respect of long distance fisheries does not provide it with precise information as to the exact extent of the maritime boundary which existed between the Parties. This issue could be expected to have been resolved by the Parties in the context of their tacit agreement and reflected in the treaty which acknowledges that tacit agreement, namely the 1954 Special Maritime Frontier Zone Agreement. This did not happen. This left some uncertainty as to the precise length of the agreed maritime boundary. However, based on an assessment of the entirety of the relevant evidence presented to it, the Court concludes that the agreed maritime boundary between the Parties extended to a distance of 80 nautical miles along the parallel from its starting-point.

(a) Practice of the parties: hunting and fishing

The parties did not provide the Court with detailed information about their fishing and hunting activities in their respective maritime zones. The information they did provide was designed to set out the

reasons that prompted them to issue their respective unilateral proclamations in 1947 and, later on, to adopt the *Santiago Declaration*
in 1952 (PM:58–60; 105–107; CCM:109–115). Chile's Counter Memorial included additional data on fishing in order to underscore the
economic benefits that Peru had derived from having a stable lateral boundary for more than sixty years (CCM:109–115). This data,
however, was neither systematic nor comprehensive, and the parties
would not have expected the Court to use it to determine the extent
of the lateral boundary. Yet, the Court deemed it sufficient and there
is no indication that it made any attempt to gather evidence from any
other source. Thus, relying on limited information, the Court concluded that the principal activity in the area was fishing carried out
by small vessels (#109) and that 'the species which were taken in the
early 1950s were generally to be found within a range of 60 nautical
miles from the coast' (#108). Because of the orientation of the coast,
the Court added another 20 nm to the boundary, thus arriving at the
80 nm figure (#108). As already noted, the Court does not provide
information about the size of the so-called 'small vessels' and entirely
ignores whale hunting, which was an important activity at the time.

I) SMALL VESSELS

The Court's finding that the lateral boundary was only 80 nm was
based on the supposition that only small vessels operated in the area
(##109, 117, 149, 151). Yet, the Court provides no information about
the precise size of vessels. In paragraph 103, it notes that fishing by
small vessels of the type mentioned in the *Special Agreement* was only
one of the elements of the practice that it would consider. Later, in
paragraph 109, the Court states that:

> [T]he catch figures indicate that the principal maritime activity
> in the early 1950s was fishing undertaken by small vessels, such
> as those specifically mentioned in the 1954 Special Maritime
> Frontier Zone Agreement and which were also to benefit from the
> 1968–1969 arrangements relating to the lighthouses.

From this data, the Court infers that the only vessels operating in the
area in the mid-1950s were small vessels, similar to those benefiting
from the exemption established by the *Special Agreement*. The Court's
supposition begs a crucially important question. If the only vessels
operating in the area were small vessels, of the type mentioned in the
Special Agreement, why would the parties have taken the trouble to

establish an exceptional regime for small vessels? It is simply not credible that they would have established a special regime for small vessels
if no other type of vessels operated in the area. The Court failed to
notice that a fundamental assumption of the *Special Agreement* was
that large and small vessels were involved in fishing and whale hunting
in the area.

II) WHALE HUNTING

The Court's inquiry into the practice of the parties did not take into
account whale hunting. The reason it ignored this activity is set out in
paragraph 107:

> The Parties also referred to the hunting of whales by their fleets
> and by foreign fleets as one of the factors leading to the adoption
> of the 1947 and 1952 instruments. The FAO [Food and Agriculture
> Organization] statistics provide some information about the ex-
> tent of whale catches by the Parties; there is no indication of where
> those catches occurred.

The fact that the FAO statistics do not indicate the location of whale
hunting is not a reason for ignoring this important activity. It is all the
more surprising that whale hunting is ignored since the Court cited a
statement by Peru's Foreign Minister in which he notes that 'the cach-
alot and whales were usually to be found more than 100 miles off [the
coast]' (#106). The Court also acknowledged that, in 1954, Peru seized
five of eleven vessels of the Onassis whaling fleet, an event which took
place between 120 and 160 nm from the coast and which also involved
pursuit of three vessels beyond 200 nm from the coast (Kunz 1956:837;
Loring 1971:404; Phleger 1955:937; Scheiber 2011:358; Sorensen
1958:214; US Naval War College 1956:290). This episode demonstrates
that Peru was capable and willing to enforce its claim way beyond the
80 nm limit established by the Court (Hollick 1978:84).

Whale hunting has a long history in the region (Grafton et al.
2010:3–19; Hollick 1977:496; Quiroz 2014). In the nineteenth and early
twentieth century, Chile and Peru attracted whaling expeditions from
a variety of countries, including the US, the UK and Norway (Flores
2011; Pastene and Quiroz 2010:88). In the twentieth century whale
hunting in Chile was undertaken mainly by Indus (*Compañia Indus-
trial*), a local company established in 1901 (for the names of other local companies involved in whaling before 1947, see, Sepúlveda 1997).
Initially involved in manufacturing chemicals, fertilizers and soaps,

Indus entered into the whaling industry in the 1930s after purchasing two factory ships. In 1943, it established a land station in the port of Quintay, in the vicinity of Valparaíso. The success of its whaling operations there led to the establishment of two additional land stations: one in the south of the country, in Talcahuano; and the other in Iquique, which is only 200 km south of the boundary with Peru. The plant in Iquique was established in 1956. Available statistics indicate that between 1944 and 1967, Indus caught 28,578 whales, most of which were sperm whales (Pastene and Quiroz 2010).

The importance of whaling for the national economy is widely acknowledged as a major factor prompting Chile's Unilateral Proclamation of 1947 claiming sovereignty over 200 nm from the coast (Hollick 1977:499; Orrego 1999:37). The choice of 200 nm is linked to the Humboldt Current System, which extends between 180 and 250 miles off the coast of Chile and provides a rich feeding ground for whales (Shapiro 1965:9; Thiel 2007; Universidad Andrés Bello 2017). Another factor explaining the 200 nm extent is that this was roughly the distance covered by land-based whale catchers (Loring 1971:400). Peru's involvement in whaling was not as intense as Chile's, but it was important enough for Peru to prevent foreign whaling fleets, such as Onassis' fleet, from entering its maritime zone (Lux 1971:142).

The economic importance of whaling explains why one of the main objectives of the 1952 Conference, which led to the adoption of the *Santiago Declaration,* was to protect this activity. Chile's letter of invitation to the Conference states that one of its purposes was 'to conclude agreements regarding the problems caused by whaling in the waters of the South Pacific and the industrialization of whale products' (PM: Annex 64; see also PR:143). At the Conference, the Chilean delegate reminded his Peruvian and Ecuadorian colleagues that more than 300 whaling vessels arrived every year at the coasts of South American countries, catching between 15,000 and 20,000 whales, and accounting for a substantial proportion of the world's production of whale oil (Kunz 1956:850). The importance of whale hunting is further confirmed by the fact that one of the four Agreements adopted by the parties at the Santiago Conference was to regulate whaling in their new maritime zones (*Regulations Governing Whaling in the Waters of the South Pacific; Reglamento para las Faenas de Caza Marítima en las Aguas del Pacífico Sur*). At the Lima Conference in 1954, the parties adopted another agreement on whale hunting (*Convention on the Ordinary Annual Meeting of the Permanent Commission for the South Pacific (for Whaling Activities); Convenio sobre la Reunión Ordinaria Anual de la Comisión Permanente del Pacífico Sur (para actividades de caza de ballenas*)). In 1955 they introduced detailed regulations to govern the granting of permits for fishing and whaling in their respective zones (*Reglamento de Permisos para la Explotación de las Riquezas del Pacífico Sur* (Comisión Permanente del Pacífico Sur 2007:83–92)). The parties' regulatory framework on whaling was acknowledged by the Food and Agriculture Organization (FAO), in 1955, as an important regional contribution to the conservation of living resources of the sea (US Naval War College 1956:215–237).

Whale hunting, a major marine activity for the parties in the early- and mid-1950s, was carried out within the 200 nm maritime zones. It was carried out by vessels with the speed and tonnage adequate to the task, not by small vessels. Thus, the seaward limit of 80 nm set by the Court for the lateral boundary is unrealistic.

III) FISHING ACTIVITIES

The Court presented its finding on the extent of the lateral boundary as the outcome of a factual inquiry into the parties' fishing activities. The information it used was taken from FAO statistics, contained mainly in Chile's written pleadings (CCM:113–116). The Court's analysis of this data is to be found in paragraph 107 of the Judgment:

> Chile referred the Court to statistics produced by the Food and Agricultural Organization of the United Nations (FAO) to demonstrate the extent of the fishery activities of Chile and Peru in the early 1950s and later years for the purpose of showing, as Chile saw the matter, the benefits of the 1952 Santiago Declaration to Peru. Those statistics reveal two facts which the Court sees as helpful in identifying the maritime areas with which the Parties were concerned in the period when they acknowledged the existence of their maritime boundary. The first is the relatively limited fishing activity by both Chile and Peru in the early 1950s. In 1950, Chile's catch at about 90,000 tonnes was slightly larger than Peru's at 74,000 tonnes. In the early 1950s, the Parties' catches of anchovy were exceeded by the catch of other species. In 1950, for instance, Peru's take of anchovy was 500 tonnes, while its catch of tuna and bonito was 44,600 tonnes; Chile caught 600 tonnes of anchovy that year, and 3,300 tonnes of tuna and bonito.
>
> Second, in the years leading up to 1954, the Parties' respective catches in the Pacific Ocean included large amounts of bonito/barrilete and tuna. While it is true that through the 1950s the take of anchovy, especially by Peru, increased very rapidly, the catch of

the other species continued at a high and increasing level. In 1954 the Peruvian catch of tuna and bonito was 65,900, and of anchovy 43,100, while Chile caught 5,200 and 1,300 tonnes of those species, respectively.

According to the Court, the statistics reveal two main facts: that the parties' fishing activity in the early 1950s was 'relatively limited'; and that, at that time, the catch of anchovy was lower than that of other species, such as tuna and bonito. These observations led the Court to conclude that fishing by both parties in the early 1950s involved only 'small vessels' (#109) with limited 'extractive capacity' (#149). Hence, it concluded, the extent of the boundary agreed by the parties could not be more than 80 nm. This conclusion is questionable on several grounds.

The statistics used by the Court record the annual catch of each country, but contain no information about fishing activities in the area close to the lateral boundary. Moreover, the Court's interpretation of these figures is confusing. According to the Court, the FAO statistics show that, in 1950, 'Chile's catch at about 90,000 tonnes was slightly larger than Peru's at 74,000 tonnes' (#107). These figures, however, do not correspond to those in Chile's Counter Memorial. Besides, the catch figures in the Counter Memorial relate to 1952, not 1950, and indicate that, in that year, Peru's catch was 106,600 metric tonnes (32,000 more than the figure attributed by the Court to Peru in 1950), while Chile's catch was 95,300 metric tonnes, a very small increase from the figure the Court assigns to Chile in 1950 (CCM:109, 111). It is also odd that the Court described Chile's catch in 1950 as 'slightly larger than Peru's' (#107), although in its Counter Memorial Chile states that its catch 'has always been smaller than Peru's' (CCM:111). Chile's statement about the size of its catch in relation to Peru's is uncontroversial, since Peru has always been a more important producer and exporter of fish products than Chile (Glantz 1979).

The figures used by the Court record Chile and Peru's overall catch and do not provide information about fishing in the vicinity of the lateral boundary. Nevertheless, on the basis of these figures, the Court concluded that fishing was 'relatively limited' in the early 1950s (#107). It is not clear, however, what the Court meant when it described the fishing activities as 'relatively limited'. Did it want to suggest that more intensive fishing would have required a lengthier boundary line? Yet, since the Court concluded that the species taken in the early 1950s, such as anchovies, 'were generally to be found within a range of 60 nautical miles from the coast' (#108), more intensive fishing would have had no bearing on the length of the boundary. Why did the Court focus on the level of activity in the early 1950s and not during the rest of that decade? Did the Court want to suggest that the parties were not interested in a more extensive boundary, either because their ambition for their respective fishing industries was modest or because they lacked the vision to safeguard their fishing interests? It seems that what the Court wanted to suggest was that the parties did not anticipate the rapid development of their fishing industry in the 1950s and beyond. If this interpretation is correct, it would explain why the parties, giving up more than half of their 200 nm claim, settled for a lateral boundary of merely 80 nm. The evidence, however, does not support this interpretation.

Evidence from several sources confirm that fishing and hunting activities were economically important long before the parties made their respective Unilateral Proclamations in 1947 (Doucet and Einarsson 1966). The Peruvian Government established a Department of Fisheries in 1943 to support every aspect of fish production, including marketing (Lux 1971:139). Commercial fishing was well under way in the 1940s with some 26 million pounds of fishery products landed in Peruvian ports (Fiedler 1944:101). In a report on Chile for the US Department of the Interior, Sidney Shapiro, noted that, during the 1950s, the State Development Corporation (CORFO) invested 30 million dollars in fish reduction, canning and freezing installations (Shapiro 1965:1).

During the Second World War, Peru supplied salt fish to the United States and after the war it exported canned fish (Horna 1968:394). Its most successful export was fishmeal, made largely from anchovy and used as fodder for poultry, pigs and cattle in the US and Europe (Glantz 1979:201; see also, Hollick 1977:499). Peru's fishmeal exports began in 1947, but its full potential was not realized until the 1950s, when fishmeal producers overcame the resistance of local guano producers, who had lobbied to protect anchovies, the main feed for guano-producing birds (Glantz 1979:205). Tension among different interests in Peru might explain why the anchovy catch, as recorded by the Court, was slow to take off in the 1950s. By the early 1950s, however, fishing was already established as an important industry in Peru, as confirmed by the FAO statistics cited in a paper by Eduardo Ferrero, a former Peruvian Foreign Minister. According to Ferrero, Peru's catch, at 84,000 metric tonnes, represented less than half of 1% of the world's catch in 1948, but by 1956, Peru's share, at 658,000 metric tonnes, represented just over 2.05%. From then on, Peru's share of the world's catch increased rapidly to 9% in 1960 and just under 16% in 1962 (Ferrero 1974:43). Thus, by the 1960s Peru was one of the largest fishing nations in the world

(Glantz 1979:201). Against this background, the Court's statement that the FAO statistics reveal relatively limited fishing activity by both Chile and Peru is inaccurate and fails to capture the dynamic nature of their fishing industries in the 1940s and early 1950s.

It is regrettable that the Court relied on inadequate and incomplete data to decide the critically important question of the extent of the lateral boundary. The Court's assertion that, at the time, only small vessels operated in the area is purely speculative and contradicted by the premise underlying the *Special Agreement* of 1954 that large and small vessels operated there. Moreover, the notion that the tacitly agreed boundary should be determined by the activities of small vessels is implausible because it assumes that in the early- and mid-1950s, when fishing and whale hunting were major economic activities in both countries, the parties had no interest in securing a lateral boundary that would extend the full length of their 200 nm claim. The Court also fails to take into consideration that, at the time, both Chile and Peru were implementing sound economic policies to develop and regulate their fishing and hunting activities. The Court, disregarding these facts, assumed instead that the parties lacked economic foresight, were politically irresponsible and did not take seriously the ten international agreements concluded in 1952 and 1954.

C. Contemporaneous law of the sea

1. Purpose of the inquiry

The Court's inquiry into contemporaneous developments in the law of the sea was brief (##112–116) and ostensibly intended to help it determine the extent of the tacitly agreed maritime boundary. It led the Court to the following conclusion (#117):

> On the basis of the fishing activities of the Parties at that time, which were conducted up to a distance of some 60 nautical miles from the main ports in the area, the relevant practice of other States and the work of the International Law Commission on the Law of the Sea, the Court considers that the evidence at its disposal does not allow it to conclude that the agreed maritime boundary along the parallel extended beyond 80 nautical miles from its starting-point.

The outcome of this inquiry was unconvincing. The inquiry was not based on a comprehensive analysis of state practice during the relevant period. It offered an incomplete and partly erroneous depiction of the work of the International Law Commission (ILC). It did not take into account the question of fisheries jurisdiction as a factor in the controversy over the breadth of the territorial sea. Its interpretation of the legal status of the parties' 200 nm claim was contradictory and incomplete.

It is necessary to understand the purpose of the Court's inquiry on the law of the sea in the 1950s. Its objective was to shed light on the seaward extent of the lateral boundary. It is not clear, however, whether the Court was trying to determine the kind of agreement that the parties would have concluded in the light of the constraints imposed by contemporary rules of international law. If so, it becomes clear that the inquiry was pointless, since the undisputed intention of the parties was to challenge prevailing rules on the law of the sea. As a consequence, even assuming that the Court's inquiry had unambiguously concluded that contemporaneous international law did not allow states to extend their territorial and fisheries jurisdiction beyond 3, 6 or 12 miles, it is inconceivable that this finding would have persuaded the parties to opt for a lateral boundary that was shorter than 200 nm. Thus, if contemporaneous international law did not alter the parties' commitment to the 200 nm claim, it seems that the only purpose of the inquiry was to underpin the Court's problematic finding that the seaward extension of the lateral boundary was only 80 nm. If this was the purpose, its outcome is awkward. The Court suggests that contemporaneous international law did not allow lateral boundaries to extend beyond 12 nm from the baseline; nonetheless, it found that the extension of the tacitly agreed lateral boundary was 80 nm. As a consequence, both 80 nm—favoured by the Court—and 200 nm—claimed by the parties—would have been illegal and void from the start.

2. State practice

According to the Court, its inquiry on state practice would comprise analysis of various claims from the mid-1940s to the mid-1950s, and of responses of states to the proposals of the International Law Commission on the Law of the Sea (#112). Disappointingly, however, its analysis is brief and insufficient. It consists of a long list of countries that made unilateral declarations. The list distinguishes between countries that made claims over the continental shelf from those that claimed control over the waters above the shelf, which include the claim made by the three signatories of the *Santiago Declaration* (#113). The Court does not comment on these declarations, but observes that some addressed the question of delimitation, such as the Truman Proclamation on the continental shelf, while others, including the declarations of Chile, Costa Rica and Mexico, stated that they would respect the rights of other states on the basis of reciprocity (#114). Although the Court acknowledges that these declarations served as background for the ILC Draft Articles on the Law of the Sea, it does not explain their impact in shaping the ILC's work, or the impact of the ILC's draft on the first UN Conference on the Law of the Sea in 1958. The Court also fails to discuss the response of third states to the parties' 200 nm claim other than noting the negative response by leading maritime powers. It also ignores the role of regional international organizations, such as the Organization of American States, which took a keen interest in the development of the law of the sea, a fact duly acknowledged by the ILC (YILC 1956 (II):249). In the absence of a detailed analysis of state practice, the list of unilateral proclamations identified by the Court suggests, albeit wrongly, that there was consensus on key aspects of the law of the sea from the early 1950s to the 1960s and that this consensus is reflected in the draft proposals of the ILC. The Court disregards the prevailing uncertainty and instability on most matters concerning the law of the sea.

3. Role of the International Law Commission

The ILC played a major role in shaping the legal debate on the law of the sea during the early years of the United Nations. It prepared a Draft that provided the basis for negotiations at the First Law of the Sea Conference in 1958. The Court's analysis of the ILC's Draft is, however, disappointing. It focuses on technical issues of delimitation that are not directly relevant to the case and does not offer an accurate account of the ILC's views on the breadth of the territorial sea (#115). On the question of delimitation, the Court notes that the ILC's proposals were largely accepted by Conference, as reflected in Article 12 of the *Convention on the Territorial Sea and Contiguous Zone* and Article 6 of the *Convention on the Continental Shelf*. Regarding the breadth of the territorial sea, the Court notes that, at that time:

> [T]he territorial sea was not seen by the International Law Commission, and would not have been seen at that time by most nations, as extending beyond 6 nautical miles and the continental

shelf line was for the sea-bed and subsoil, extending to a 200-metre depth or beyond to the limit of exploitability, and not for the resources of the water above the shelf.

(#115)

The Court reinforces this point observing that 'during the period under consideration, the proposal that came nearest to international acceptance was for a 6-nautical-mile territorial sea with a further fishing zone of six nautical miles and some reservations of established fishing rights' (#116).

(a) Delimitation proposals

The Court focuses on the ILC's draft on delimitation, although they were not at issue in this case. The ILC proposed that the equidistance line should be used for the delimitation of the territorial sea and continental shelf, in the absence of an agreement or special circumstance (#115). Surprisingly, however, the Court makes an additional observation on the ILC's views on the geographical parallel as a method of delimitation—the method employed in Paragraph IV of the *Santiago Declaration*. According to the Court, 'the Commission in particular rejected, in the absence of an agreement, as a basis for the line the geographical parallel passing through the point at which the land frontier meets the coast' (#115). This statement is inaccurate. The ILC did not reject this or any other method of delimitation. In its Commentary the ILC summarizes the Committee of Experts' views on various methods of delimitation.[1] The only method rejected by the Committee as impracticable, was the method that involves drawing lines at right angles to the general direction of the coastline (for example, the Brazil-Uruguay delimitation agreement of 1972 (United Nations 2000:56)). The ILC's Commentary on this method is as follows (YILC 1956 (II):272):

> The group of experts...was unable to support this last method of drawing the boundary line. It was of opinion that it was often impracticable to establish any "general direction of the coast'; the result would depend on the 'scale of the charts used for the purpose and... how much coast shall be utilized in attempting to determine any general direction whatever'.

1 For information on this committee, see YILC 1956 (II):255; for an interesting discussion of the equidistance method and the Committee of Experts, see *North Sea Continental Shelf*, Judgment, ICJ Reports 1969, 3, paragraphs 47–56.

The Committee of Experts, however, did not reject the line of the geographical parallel as a method of delimitation. The relevant passage from the ILC's Commentary reads as follows (YILC 1956 (II):272):

> [A] third solution would be to adopt as the demarcation line the geographical parallel passing through the point at which the land frontier meets the coast. This solution is not applicable in all cases either.

The ILC and the Committee of Experts undoubtedly favoured the equidistance method. More importantly, however, and contrary to the Court's observation, the ILC did not reject the use of geographical parallel as a method of delimitation. This inaccuracy would have been inconsequential had the Court not added a remark suggesting that, the parties made no comment (#115):

> The Commission in particular rejected, in the absence of an agreement, as a basis for the line the geographical parallel passing through the point at which the land frontier meets the coast. Chile and Ecuador in their observations submitted to the Commission contended that the rights of the coastal State over its continental shelf went beyond just 'control' and 'jurisdiction'; Chile, in addition, called for 'sovereignty' over both the continental shelf and superjacent waters. However, neither State made any comment on the matter of delimitation. Peru made no comment of any kind. This further supports the view that the chief concern of the three States in this period was defending their 200-nautical-mile claims as against third States.

This observation seems to suggest that the parties did not respond to ILC proposals on the geographical parallel because they had not delimited their lateral boundary. This suggestion, however, is incorrect. The parties had no reason to respond because the ILC did not reject the geographical parallel as a method of delimitation. This suggestion is also unfair because the Court, familiar as it is with ILC Reports, should have been aware that, on several occasions, Chile and Peru responded to ILC drafts. In a letter to the UN General Assembly Chile noted that

> the position of the Chilean Government in the matter of the provisional articles concerning the regime of the sea has been determined by domestic legislation, by the international agreements signed with Ecuador and Peru and by Chile's attitude in the international organizations concerned.

The letter then draws attention to the Presidential Proclamation of 1947 and the Agreements signed with Ecuador and Peru in Santiago in 1952 and in Lima in 1954. Chile also mentions various Inter-American Resolutions that had supported the parties' position on the law of the sea, as reflected in the 1952 and 1954 Agreements (YILC 1956 (II):42–43). Both Chile and Peru rejected the ILC's proposals. According to Chile they were unacceptable because there were no grounds for considering that international law does not permit an extension of the territorial sea beyond 12 nm (*United Nations Conference on the Law of the Sea 1958, Volume I:*77–79). Peru also rejected the ILC's views on the breadth of the territorial sea. In its statement Peru noted that 'each State is competent to establish its territorial waters within reasonable limits, taking into account geographical, geological and biological factors, as well as the economic needs of its population, and its security and defence' (Ibid.:97–98). The parties' response to the ILC draft does not address the question concerning methods of delimitation because neither the ILC draft nor its Commentary contained anything that could be interpreted as critical to the method employed in Paragraph IV of the *Santiago Declaration*.

(b)   Breadth of the territorial sea

In paragraph 115 the Court states that the ILC did not see the territorial sea as extending beyond 6 nm. This statement is inaccurate and confusing: inaccurate because the figure mentioned in the ILC draft to the UN General Assembly is 12 miles, not 6; and confusing because it is presented as a firm proposal for codification.[2]

Thus, to assess the Court's remarks on the views of the ILC it is necessary to examine Article 3 of the Draft that the ILC submitted to the General Assembly (YILC 1956 (II):256):

1   The Commission recognizes that international practice is not uniform as regards the delimitation of the territorial sea.
2   The Commission considers that international law does not permit an extension of the territorial sea beyond 12 miles.
3   The Commission, without taking any decision as to the breadth of the territorial sea up to that limit, notes, on the one hand, that many states have fixed a breadth greater than 3 miles and,

---

2   The term mile, as used by the ILC in its Report to the General Assembly and as used in official Law of the Sea Conference documents, means nautical mile (YILC 1956 (II):256).

on the other hand, that many states do not recognize such a breadth when that of their own territorial sea is less.

4   The Commission considers that the breadth of the territorial sea should be fixed by an international conference.

The obvious point that emerges from draft Article 3(2) is that, contrary to the Court's statement, the ILC considered that the maximum extension of the territorial sea under international law was 12, not 6 nm. A more general point is that, rather than a proposal for codification, this draft article reflects the conflicting views among ILC members on the breadth of the territorial sea (YILC 1956 (I):182). The first paragraph confirms that the practice of states on the delimitation of the territorial sea is not uniform. As a consequence, the statement in the second paragraph regarding the maximum extension of the territorial sea can only be regarded as an opinion of the majority of ILC members. An examination of the deliberations confirms that the reason why paragraph 4 proposes that an international conference should be set up to resolve the breadth of the territorial sea is because the ILC had been unable to agree on this important question (Jessup 1955; Sorensen 1958:243). The ILC accepted Commissioner Gerald Fitzmaurice's suggestion that, given the disagreement on this point, the ILC should 'inform the General Assembly that it could not state what the rule was' (YILC 1956 (I):175). Further evidence of the ILC's position with regard to provisions of Article 3 is found in its Commentary of draft Article 3. Here the ILC notes that it had rejected a proposal calling for disputes over the breadth of the territorial sea to be submitted to the compulsory jurisdiction of the International Court of Justice, because 'the majority of [the members of] the Commission …were unwilling to ask the Court to undertake the settlement of disputes on a subject regarding which the international community had not yet succeeded in formulating a rule of law' (YILC 1956 (II):266). As a consequence, there can be little doubt that the reference to a maximum extension of 12 nm—or six if we follow the Court's interpretation—was not an authoritative statement of the law. While undoubtedly, at the time, most members of ILC did not endorse extensive maritime claims such as those made by Chile, Ecuador and Peru, it would be wrong to conclude that, in the mid-1950s there was a generally accepted customary rule on the breadth of the territorial sea. The early- and mid-1950s were a time of great uncertainty on all matters relating to the law of the sea, especially on issues regarding the breadth of the territorial sea and fisheries jurisdiction.

The uncertainty on matters relating to the law of the sea is evident in articles published by three prominent contemporary observers before they became judges of the International Court of Justice—Jens Evensen, Richard Baxter and Humphrey Waldock. They all agreed that the matter of the breadth of the territorial sea could not be resolved either by applying traditional legal doctrine, such as the 3-mile rule, or by referral to the International Court of Justice. Jens Evensen, writing in 1952, acknowledged that traditional law of the sea doctrines were seriously challenged by a flood of new maritime claims and correctly predicted that 'many of the newly promulgated laws and regulations would soon prove valid and justified in international law' (Evensen 1952:628). Four years later, Professor Richard Baxter, acknowledging that the practice of states on the breadth of the territorial sea had undergone a significant evolution, called upon the United States to abandon its rigid adherence to the 3-mile rule doctrine and adopt instead a policy more in tune with the trends of the time (Baxter 1956:117, 124). In 1956 Professor Waldock, after critically reviewing a range of new maritime claims, came to the conclusion that it was time for an international conference to resolve this matter (Waldock 1956:193). The uncertainty prevailing at the time is also reflected in the preface to the draft articles that the ILC submitted to the General Assembly. In this document the ILC wonders whether, given the volatility of state practice, it is realistic to expect legal rules to resolve the impasse. It therefore recommends the General Assembly to convene an international conference to consider not only the legal aspects of the law of the sea, but also technical, biological, economic and political aspects (YILC 1956 (II):255). Thus, the views of three prominent scholars and the stance of the ILC confirm the prevailing uncertainty concerning the law of the sea, particularly, on the matter of the breadth of the territorial sea. The Court's remarks on the ILC's draft articles fail to take these concerns into account.

4. *Territorial sea and fisheries jurisdiction*

(a) An ambiguous statement

Upon concluding its discussion of the work of the ILC, the Court remarks on the breadth of the territorial sea and fisheries jurisdiction. This remark, paragraph 116, requires careful consideration as it is the most ambiguous paragraph in this Judgment (#116):

> The Court observes that, during the period under consideration, the proposal in respect of the rights of a State over its waters which came nearest to general international acceptance was for a 6-nautical-mile territorial sea with a further fishing zone of

6 nautical miles and some reservation of established fishing rights. As the Court has noted previously, in this period the concept of an exclusive economic zone of 200 nautical miles was 'still some long years away' (*Maritime Delimitation in the Black Sea (Romania v. Ukraine), Judgment, I.C.J. Reports 2009*, p. 87, para. 70), while its general acceptance in practice and in the 1982 United Nations Convention on the Law of the Sea was about 30 years into the future. In answering a question from a Member of the Court, both Parties recognized that their claim made in the 1952 Santiago Declaration did not correspond to the international law of that time and was not enforceable against third parties, at least not initially.

On the surface, the three sentences in this paragraph are strictly descriptive. The first recalls the six-plus-six formula, which was a proposal on the territorial sea and fisheries jurisdiction that gained considerable support at the Law of the Sea Conferences in 1958 and 1960. The second states that the Exclusive Economic Zone (EEZ) was approved by the Third International Law of the Sea Conference in 1982. The third recounts the parties' answer to a question from the bench. What is striking about this paragraph is that, while none of the three sentences purports to make an authoritative statement about the law of the sea in the early and mid-1950s, when read together they acquire a curious normative quality. The underlying message is that the 200 nm claim was void *ab initio* and invalid *erga omnes*. Yet, nowhere in the Judgment does the Court make this statement.

It is interesting to consider how the Court extracts normative content from three factual statements, thus enabling it to avoid making a clear statement on the legal status of the 200 nm claim. The first sentence evokes the well-known fact that, at the 1958 and 1960 Law of the Sea Conferences, the proposal that 'came nearest to international acceptance was for a 6-nautical-mile territorial sea with a further fishing zone of 6 nautical miles...'. The Court then recalls that during the relevant period the notion of an exclusive economic zone had not yet been universally accepted. This statement is historically correct, but its presentation is curiously elaborate:

> [A]s the Court has noted previously, in this period the concept of an exclusive economic zone of 200 nautical miles was 'still some long years away' (*Maritime Delimitation in the Black Sea (Romania v. Ukraine), Judgment, I.C.J. Reports 2009*, p. 87, para. 70), while its general acceptance in practice and in the 1982 United Nations Convention on the Law of the Sea was about 30 years into the future.

The reference to the *Romania v. Ukraine* case is superfluous.[3] Yet, the shift from an innocuous statement about the six-plus-six formula in the first sentence to a factual statement that, unnecessarily, invokes the *Romania v. Ukraine case* can only be interpreted as an oblique attempt to insinuate that the parties' 200 nm claim was invalid. This interpretation is confirmed by the third sentence of paragraph 116. In this paragraph the Court relies on statements made by the parties in order to convey a message it seems reluctant to make with its own voice: 'both Parties recognized that their claim made in the 1952 Santiago Declaration did not correspond to the international law of that time and was not enforceable against third parties, at least not initially'.

The elusiveness of this paragraph is more frequently encountered in political discourse than in judicial settings. In order to understand its ambiguity, it is necessary to examine two areas of the law of the sea that the Court did not examine: the status of the six-plus-six formula and the critical question concerning the enforceability of the 200 nm claim.

(b) The six-plus-six formula

The prolonged deadlock over the breadth of the territorial sea stemmed largely from disagreements over fisheries. This deadlock was resolved in 1982 by the *United Nations Law of the Sea Convention* (UNCLOS), which provides that the territorial sea extends to a maximum of 12 nm, the contiguous zone to a maximum of 24 nm and the Exclusive

---

3 It should be noted that during the litigation the parties discussed the *Romania v. Ukraine case*. At the oral hearings Peru invoked the Court's Judgment in *Romania v. Ukraine* in order to reject Chile's argument that the *Santiago Declaration* had established the lateral boundary. According to Peru, in 1952, the parties could not have defined any type of boundary, let alone one that included the continental shelf and the Exclusive Economic Zone, because at the time, these zones were not yet recognised by international law. Peru cited two statements made by the Court in *Romania v. Ukraine*: the statement that in 1949 the concept of the EEZ 'was still some long years away' (*Compte Rendu* 2012/27:51(Treves)); and the statement that Romania and Ukraine 'would be expected to conclude a new agreement' since at the relevant time the EEZ did not exist as a concept (*Compte Rendu* 2012/33:55 (Treves)). Chile queried the relevance of the *Romania v. Ukraine* judgment. It pointed out that what was at issue in that case was whether an agreement meant to delimit the territorial boundary up to 12 miles from the coast could also be applied to the parties' continental shelf and exclusive economic zone. By contrast, in this dispute, the parties had delimited their maritime zones and the zones they established were 'historically continuous with those that exist today' (*Compte Rendu* 2012/36:38/9 (Crawford)).

Economic Zone (EEZ) to a maximum of 200 nm from the baseline (UNCLOS, Articles 3, 33 and 57).

The first Law of the Sea Conference, despite failing to resolve the question of the breadth of the territorial sea, managed to make some progress. It approved the 1958 *Convention on the Territorial Sea and Contiguous Zone,* which established the contiguous zone (Article 24) extending to a maximum of 12 nm from the baseline, thus implying a maximum limit for the territorial sea. The contiguous zone, however, was not an alternative to the fisheries zone. It was meant to prevent infringement of customs, fiscal and other regulations. An important development during the mid-1950s, was that Chile and Peru began to shift their position emphasising that the objective of their maritime claim was to exercise jurisdiction and control over fisheries, rather than to extend their territorial sea (Zacklin 1974:62–63). Indeed, in 1955 when the CEP countries held direct negotiations with the United States over their 200 nm claim, they made a proposal that introduced a distinction between the 12 nm territorial sea and maritime zones beyond the territorial sea. They also focused their attention on issues concerning fisheries jurisdiction and conservation (Baxter 1956:124; Phleger 1955; US Department of State 1955; US Department of State (Mimeo) 1955). The following year, in statements before the Sixth (Legal) Committee of the General Assembly, Chile and Peru reiterated the view that their 200 nm claim was mainly aimed at controlling and conserving natural resources (PR: Annex 58 and 59; see also García Sayan 1974:11). The Court briefly alluded to these statements, but failed to note that the parties were primarily interested in controlling natural resources, rather than extending their territorial sea (#106). At the 1958 Law of the Sea Conference, Chile and Peru again reiterated that their objective was to extend their jurisdiction over the living resources in order to conserve these resources and further their development objectives. This is why they strongly objected to the ILC's definition of the high seas which, ignoring their claim to jurisdiction over a maritime zone beyond the territorial sea, envisaged unrestricted freedom of fishing on the high seas. (See speech by Peru's delegate Dr Garcia Sayan in *Official Records of the United Nations Conference on the Law of the Sea, 1958, Volume IV,* pp. 17–18. Similar views were expressed by Mr. Gutierrez-Olivos, the Chilean delegate, *Official Records of the United Nations Conference on the Law of the Sea, 1958,* Volume III, pp. 32–33).

Responding to these developments, the United States proposed, in 1958, a compromise formula that recognised a special fisheries zone for coastal states. The compromise envisaged a 6 nm territorial sea and a contiguous and exclusive fisheries zone of a further 6 nm, subject to the preservation of rights of states that had fished in that area during the previous five years (*United Nations Conference on the Law of the Sea, Official Records, 1958*, Vol. III, pp. 153, 163, 253). The objective of this proposal, which came to be known as the six-plus-six proposal, was to reconcile the interests of coastal states with the interests of states with longstanding fishing interests outside their own territorial sea. Although this attempt failed, the United States again tried to break the deadlock in 1960. This new proposal reiterated the six-plus-six formula, but gave coastal states exclusive fishing rights in the contiguous zone and established a ten-year time limit for the preservation of the rights of other states that had fished in the area (*Second United Nations Conference on the Law of the Sea 1960*:20–22, 29–30, 45–46, 121–122, 166–167, 173). This new proposal, co-sponsored by Brazil, Canada, Cuba and the United Kingdom, enjoyed considerable support, but failed, by one vote, to secure the required two-third majority (Dean 1960:751; for a detailed analysis of this process, see Bowett 1960). As a consequence, after two successive Law of the Sea Conferences, it became clear that, although the territorial sea and the fisheries zones were legally different issues, there could be no agreement on the breadth of the territorial sea, unless the question over fisheries was settled. Prominent academic observers also acknowledged that issues over the breadth of the territorial sea and fisheries would continue to create complications well into the future (Bowett 1960:434–435; Brierly 1963:210–211; Gros 1959:83).

(c) The 1958 Fisheries Convention

In 1958, the Law of the Sea Conference adopted the *Convention on Fishing and Conservation of the Living Resources of the High Seas*. Neither Chile nor Peru signed up to this Convention because it did not recognize that coastal states had jurisdiction and control over the living resources of the sea beyond the—as yet unspecified—territorial sea (Bishop 1962:1207). In their view, the policy underlying this Convention was in sharp contrast to the approach taken by the 1958 *Convention on the Continental Shelf*, which recognized that coastal states have sovereign rights for the purpose of exploring and exploiting mineral and other non-living resources of the seabed and subsoil (Article 2). Since Chile and Peru had strong fishing and hunting interests and virtually no continental shelf, they strongly criticized the inconsistency between the two Conventions. Their critical views on this Convention were eloquently expressed by Mr. Letts, the Peruvian delegate: (*UN Conference on the Law of the Sea 1958, Volume 6*:10):

> The International Law Commission had applied very different principles to two similar situations; it had recognized the sovereign right of the coastal State to exploit mineral resources, principally oil, which could only be exploited by industrialized countries, but not similarly sovereign rights over the living resources of the sea, on which many coastal States depended for the livelihood of their people. The right of unrestricted fishing on the high seas had been founded on the belief that the living resources of the sea were inexhaustible; but modern fishing methods had disproved that view, and there was therefore no longer any basis for unrestricted fishing rights. His delegation considered that it was only logical that States claiming rights over the continental shelf should also claim rights over the superjacent waters.

In the event, the 1958 *Fisheries Convention* was unsuccessful, thus paving the way for the introduction of the Exclusive Economic Zone in 1982. One of the reasons it failed was because it attempted to secure the conservation of living resources through bilateral arrangements between interested parties. It defined conservation as 'the aggregate of the measures rendering possible the optimum sustainable yield from those resources so as to secure a maximum supply to food and other marine products' (Article 2). While the Convention recognized, albeit imprecisely, that coastal states have a special interest in maintaining the productivity of the living resources in the high seas (Article 6(1)), it required states whose nationals were engaged in fishing the same stock of fish to negotiate conservation agreements based upon scientific data on the optimum sustainable yield (Article 4). This provision, designed to protect the interests of distant-water fishing fleets, proved unsuccessful because it soon became clear that scientific considerations could not override social and political considerations (Finley 2009; Finley and Oreskes 2013). As a consequence, even the United States, the most fervent proponent of the scientific approach, eventually conceded that bilateral fishery arrangements were not an adequate solution to conservation. Thus, in 1976 the US Congress adopted the *Fishery Conservation and Management Act*, extending United States fishery jurisdiction to 200 nm (Magnuson 1977; Young 1982). This Act, a belated vindication of the objectives of the *Santiago Declaration* of 1952, was based on the notion that the management and conservation of fishing resources should be the responsibility of coastal states, as they have a long-term interest in these resources. The adoption of this Act contributed to galvanizing international consensus, leading, in 1982, to the establishment of the Exclusive Economic Zone as an area adjacent to the territorial sea with a maximum extension of 200 nm (Eckert 1979:128–133). Within the EEZ, coastal states have sovereign rights for the exploration and exploitation of the natural resources found in the waters superjacent to the seabed and of the seabed and its subsoil (UNCLOS Articles 55 and 57). Coastal states have responsibility for the conservation and management of the resources within the EEZ, taking into account 'the best scientific evidence available' (UNCLOS Article 61(2)).

5. The 200 mile claim

(a) Validity and enforceability

When in 1952 the CEP countries proclaimed exclusive sovereignty and jurisdiction over the sea to a minimum distance of 200 nm from their coasts, they were conscious that their claim defied prevailing rules on the law of the sea. This is why two years later they held another conference to strengthen the legitimacy of their claim and to adopt measures to confront political and legal challenges from third parties, mainly from the United States. During this litigation, the question concerning the legality of the *Santiago Declaration* was raised by Peru. Its objective was to demonstrate that, because at the time the 200 nm claim was not universally recognized, Paragraph IV of the *Santiago Declaration* could not have validly delimited its lateral boundary. Peru's concern with the validity of the 200 nm claim is reflected in the question from the Bench, formulated by Judge Bennouna and addressed to both parties:

> Do you consider that, as signatories of the Santiago Declaration in 1952, you could at that date, in conformity with general international law, proclaim and delimit a maritime zone of sovereignty and exclusive jurisdiction over the sea that washes upon the coasts of your respective countries up to a minimum distance of 200 miles from those coasts?

In paragraph 116 the Court recalls the answer of the parties to a question from the Bench:

> In answering a question from a Member of the Court, both Parties recognized that their claim made in the 1952 Santiago Declaration

did not correspond to the international law of that time and was not enforceable against third parties, at least not initially.

Although this sentence merely summarizes the parties' response to the question, it gives the impression that the Court agrees with their views, in particular with the notion that the claim was not 'initially' enforceable. The Court, however, does not explain what the parties meant when they described the claim as not 'initially' enforceable. Did they mean that the claim was not 'instantly' enforceable? Was this because it was such a novel claim? Or, did they mean that at some point between 1952 and 1982 the claim became enforceable? In order to answer these questions it is necessary to examine the parties' responses more closely.

Peru's response to the question from the Bench was clear. It stated that the parties could proclaim and delimit the 200 nm maritime zone, but this would not have been in conformity with contemporaneous international law and would not have been opposable to third states (*Compte Rendu* 2012/33:53 (Treves)). Chile's view was that the parties could claim and delimit their new maritime zone, but this only had legal effect between the parties and was not enforceable against third parties (*Compte Rendu* 2012/35:34/5 (Dupuy)). Although these answers are incomplete (more on this below), it is helpful to recall how the parties addressed this issue.

In their written pleadings the parties disagreed over the question concerning the status of the 200 nm claim under international law. During the three decades following the *Santiago Declaration,* Peru vigorously defended the legality of the claim and resolutely enforced it, preventing distant fishing vessels, unless duly authorised by Peruvian authorities, from carrying out fishing or hunting activities in its 200 nm zone. In this litigation, however, Peru backtracked. It argued that the claim was merely a policy statement without legal force (PM:123, 127, 132). Six judges—President Tomka and Judges Skotnikov, Xue, Gaja, Bhandari and ad hoc Judge Orrego Vicuña—agreed with Chile's view that, *inter se,* the parties could delimit their lateral boundary. Judge Skotnikov clearly stated the position:

> [E]stablishing a maritime boundary between the Parties in the early 1950s to a distance of 200 nautical miles could only be understood as an agreement *inter partes*, enforceable primarily *inter se*. It is difficult to see why this would be more controversial than the 200-nautical-mile claims in the 1947 Proclamations and in the 1952 Santiago Declaration, which purport to create maritime zones to be defended against third States.
>
> (Skotnikov #4)

The Court acknowledges, in several sections of the Judgment, that the 200 nm claim had legal consequences. Had the Court deemed that the *Santiago Declaration* was void *ab initio*, because of the supposed illegality of the 200 nm claim, it would not have assumed jurisdiction. This point was forcefully made by President Tomka in his Declaration (Tomka #6). Moreover, although the Court concluded that Paragraph IV had not delimited the entire lateral boundary, it did, nonetheless, acknowledge that the *Santiago Declaration* had delimited the 200 nm maritime zones of islands and the general maritime zone generated by the continent in the event of an overlap with the respective zones of islands (#60). The Court also acknowledged that the *Santiago Declaration* together with the parties' respective Unilateral Proclamations of 1947 had determined the nature of the boundary as an all-purpose boundary. This boundary included maritime areas, such as the continental shelf, which had not yet been recognised under international law. The Court also accepted that the parties had tacitly agreed to a lateral boundary extending up to 80 nm, which is well beyond the 12 nm limit that the Court regards as the maximum extension of the territorial sea and fisheries jurisdiction allowed by contemporaneous international law. Thus, the Court accepts that in their international agreements and in their practice the parties—challenging prevailing legal concepts—adopted *inter se* legal rules to govern their relations. Yet, when it decided on the extent of the lateral boundary, it disregarded the 200 nm claim.

The Court relies on the parties' response to the question from the Bench to suggest that the 200 nm claim did not correspond to contemporaneous international law and was thus not enforceable against third parties (#116). The key issue, however, is not whether the claim was generally enforceable, but whether, and under what conditions it would have been opposable to third states. This question was considered by the Court in the 1974 *Fisheries Jurisdiction Cases (Fisheries Jurisdiction (United Kingdom v. Iceland),* Merits, Judgment, ICJ Reports 1974, 3 and *Fisheries Jurisdiction (Federal Republic of Germany v. Iceland),* Merits, Judgment, ICJ Reports 1974, 175). What was at issue in these cases was whether Iceland's extension of its fisheries zone beyond 12 nm was unfounded under international law, as claimed by the United Kingdom and Germany. The Court refrained from ruling on this point, finding instead, on the basis of agreements in force, that Iceland's decision was not opposable either to the UK or to Germany. It should be noted that in these cases the Court acknowledged that neither the 1958 nor the 1960 Law of the Sea Conferences had resolved either the question of the territorial sea or the question of the extent of the fisheries jurisdiction. It also acknowledged that the first two Law of the Sea Conferences had brought about a gradual separation of the question of fisheries from the question of the territorial sea (*Fisheries Jurisdiction (United Kingdom v. Iceland), I.C.J.* Reports 1974, paragraph #51, pp. 22–23). After recalling the near-agreement at the 1960 Conference, the Court notes, with regard to the concept of the fisheries zone, that the extension of the zone up to a 12 nm limit from the baseline 'appears now to be generally accepted' (Ibid., paragraph #52, p. 23). The Court, however, also noted that the question of fisheries and conservation of the living resources of the sea remained unsettled and strongly endorsed the decision to resolve it at the diplomatic level (at the Third Law of the Sea Conference) because 'the rules of international maritime law have been the product of mutual accommodation, reasonableness and co-operation. So it was in the past, and so it necessarily is today' (Ibid., paragraph #53, p. 23).

Any ambiguity concerning the status of the 12 nm limit was dispelled by the Joint Separate Opinion of Judges Forster, Bengzon, Jimenez de Arechaga, Nagendra Singh and Ruda. In their Separate Opinion the five judges categorically state that the 12 nm limit was not an obligatory maximum. 'There is not today an international usage to that effect sufficiently widespread and uniform as to constitute, within the meaning of Article 38, paragraph 1 (b), of the Court's Statute, "evidence of a general practice accepted as law"' (Ibid.:45). They acknowledge that an exclusive fishery zone of 12 miles had become a feature of international law since the 1958 Law of the Sea Conference and that it was respected by distant water fishing fleets. They did not, however, regard 12 nm as a maximum limit. In their view,

> to recognize the possibility that States might claim without risk of challenge or objection an exclusive fisheries zone of 12 miles cannot by any sense of logic necessarily lead to the conclusion contended for by the Applicant, namely, that such a figure constitutes in the present state of maritime international law an obligatory maximum limit and that a State going beyond such a limit commits an unlawful act, which is invalid *erga omnes.*
>
> (Ibid.:47)

The applicants in the *Fisheries cases* had argued that an extension of the fishery zone beyond 12 nm was *ipso jure* illegal and therefore invalid *erga omnes*. The Court, as noted above, did not address this contention, but Sir Humphrey Waldock, in his Separate Opinion, offers a brief and lucid explanation as to why Iceland's extension of its maritime zone from 12 to 50 nm could not be regarded as absolutely invalid under international law. In his view, given the variety of different maritime claims, the legal issue was not one of absolute legality, or illegality, of the claim, but rather a question of acceptance or acquiescence by other states. 'Therefore, an extension of fisheries jurisdiction beyond 12 nm is not, in my opinion, opposable to another State unless shown to have been accepted or acquiesced in by that state' (Ibid.:120). Following Judge Waldock's reasoning in the *Fisheries Jurisdiction cases,* the 200 nm claim was opposable to third states that recognised it, either explicitly or implicitly. Conversely, the claim would not have been opposable to states that did not recognize it, which at the time included the leading maritime powers of the day.

The foregoing also helps to clarify what the parties meant when they said that the claim was not initially enforceable (#116). This qualifying phrase was used by Chile in response to the question from the bench. In his response Chile's advocate stated that

> while the intention was for the treaties to be enforceable against third parties, that objective was clearly not achieved, *at least not initially,* as we have just seen from the salvo of protests with which they were greeted. (Author's emphasis).
>
> (*Compte Rendu* 2012/35:34/5 (Dupuy))

The implication of this statement seems to be that the 'salvo of protests' had the effect of making the claim absolutely illegal (illegal *erga omnes*), a point also made by Peru in its written pleadings (PM:71, 98, 111; PR:144/5, 158). Thus, the agreement between Chile and Peru on the question of the enforceability of the 200 nm claim was convenient, as it enabled the Court to transcribe the views of the parties without having to take a clear position on this issue (for Peru's response see *Compte Rendu* 2012/33:53 (Treves) and *Compte Rendu* 2012/27:51 (Treves)). That the Court refrained from making a clear statement about the legal status of the 200 nm claim is not surprising, since it was surely aware that Judge Waldock's Separate Opinion in the *Fisheries Jurisdiction cases* stated a widely accepted principle of international law: 'an extension of fisheries jurisdiction beyond 12 miles is not, in my opinion, opposable to another State unless shown to have been accepted or acquiesced in by that state'. Thus, in order to determine whether the 200 nm claim was opposable to other states it is necessary to focus on the response to the claim by third states.

(b) Protests, acceptance and acquiescence

The so-called 'salvo of protests', mentioned by Chile's counsel, were largely protests from the United States, the United Kingdom, Denmark, Norway and Sweden (CCM:133; see also Selak 1950:674; Loring 1971:401). By contrast, however, the majority of states in Latin America, either directly or indirectly accepted the claim. The evidence shows that from the early 1950s most countries in the region considered the prevailing rules on the territorial sea as inadequate and believed that, depending on their particular circumstances, coastal states had the right to extend their maritime jurisdiction (US Naval War College 1956:238). In July 1952, one month before the adoption of the *Santiago Declaration*, the Inter-American Juridical Committee prepared a *Draft Convention on Territorial Waters and related Questions* which provided, inter alia, that signatory states 'recognize the right of each of them to establish an area of protection, control, and economic exploitation, to a distance of two hundred nautical miles from the low-water mark along its coasts...' (Ibid.). In February 1956, the Inter-American Council of Jurists adopted the *Principles of Mexico on the Juridical Regime of the Sea,* reiterating the widely held view among states in the region that the 3-mile rule as the limit of the territorial sea was not a general rule of international law. *The Principles of Mexico* also proclaimed that 'each State is competent to establish its territorial waters within reasonable limits, taking into account geographical, geological, and biological factors, as well as the economic needs of its population, and its security and defence' (Ibid.:245). As the ILC noted in its *Report on Co-operation with Inter-American Bodies* the majority of states in Latin American rejected the 3-mile rule (eleven out of twenty-one), six other states declared that they would accept as the breadth of the territorial sea whatever the Council of Jurists or the specialized Conference would decide and four states, including the United States, took the view that there should be a 3-mile rule (YILC 1956 (II):236–252). According to the Report most of the participants to the Conference in Mexico endorsed Judge Alejandro Alvarez's Separate Opinion in the *Anglo-Norwegian Fisheries case*. In his Opinion Judge Alvarez stated that given the variety of geographical and political conditions it was not possible to apply a single rule to determine the extent of the territorial sea (Ibid.:240). In his view, each state may determine the extent of its territorial sea

provided it does so in a reasonable manner, that it is capable of exercising supervision over the zone in question and of carrying out the duties imposed by international law, that it does not infringe rights acquired by other States, that it does no harm to general interests and does not constitute an *abus de droit.*

(*Fisheries case (United Kingdom v. Norway),*
Judgment, I.C.J. Reports 1951, 116, Individual
Opinion of Judge Alvarez, 145 at 150)

In 1958, at the start of the first Law of the Sea Conference, the majority of Latin American countries regarded the 3-mile rule as inadequate. They did not, however, have a unified position on the extent of the territorial sea or the fishery zone (US Naval War College 1956:255/6). Nonetheless, they were all aware that Chile, Peru and Ecuador had made a 200 nm claim and yet no Latin American country lodged a protest. The absence of protest from other countries in the region is not surprising since most of them had made claims inconsistent with the views of the leading maritime powers (See, *Extent of Jurisdiction Claimed over the Territorial Sea, the Contiguous Zone and the Continental Shelf: Synoptical Table,* prepared by the UN Secretariat for the 1958 UN Law of the Sea Conference, US Naval College 1959/60:273–287). By the mid-1950s, the countries that had officially challenged the views of the leading maritime powers on the territorial sea and fisheries jurisdiction included Argentina, Costa Rica, El Salvador, Honduras, Mexico, Nicaragua, Panama, Venezuela as well as the three signatories of the *Santiago Declaration.* Countries from other regions also claiming extensive jurisdiction over water resources, beyond the 3-mile territorial sea, included Iceland, India, Indonesia, South Korea and the Philippines (Dean 1960:763–764). Since none of these countries protested it should be assumed that the 200 nm claim was opposable to them.

In the early 1970s, before the Third Law of the Sea Conference, support for the 200 nm claim strengthened in Latin America as several countries, including Argentina, Brazil and Uruguay, made similar claims (Martens 1976:537). The regional consensus on the question of coastal states jurisdiction was further consolidated by Resolutions adopted at three inter-governmental conferences: in Montevideo and Lima in 1970 and Santo Domingo in 1972 (García-Amador 1974; Kraska 2011:137; Zacklin 1974:66).

(c) The claim endures

One of the grounds the Court invoked to justify its finding that the lateral boundary could not extend more than 80 nm was that the 'extractive and enforcement capacity' of the parties did not extend beyond this point (#149). Yet, despite its efforts to ignore the 200 nm claim, the Court could not ignore that the parties had consistently upheld it and vigorously enforced it, issuing permits to fish or hunt in their respective maritime zones and seizing fishing vessels that entered their respective maritime zones without their permission. The parties were not only keen to generate solidarity in support of their claim, but also employed a variety of political, diplomatic and legal means to uphold and enforce their claim. Data from a 1972 Report of the Secretary General of the Permanent Commission of the South Pacific on Infractions in the Maritime Zone—cited by the Court in paragraph 127—show that between 1951 and 1971 the signatories of the *Santiago Declaration* arrested 180 fishing vessels that had not secured the appropriate permissions to fish or hunt in the 200 nm zone. The majority of the arrests, 122, were carried out by Ecuador; Peru arrested 53 and Chile five. These arrests demonstrate that the signatories of the *Santiago Declaration* had political will and ample capacity to enforce their claim well beyond 80 nm (Kraska 2011:98; Meyer 1972; Wiegand 1969:428). The Court, however, did not consider these enforcement activities had any bearing on its finding on the extent of the boundary (#129). In sharp contrast, the contemporary response of the United States to the CEP countries' policies was not complacent. It took the 200 nm claim very seriously. It deployed a range of political, diplomatic, economic and legal strategies to persuade the CEP countries to abandon their claim (Meron 1975; Meyer 1972). It enacted retaliatory legislation (Loring 1971; Pineo 2007:176–177; Weissberg 1967), attempted to submit the issue to the ICJ (Phleger 1955:934), engaged in direct negotiation with the three CEP countries, tried to drive a wedge between them using political pressure and threatening to cut foreign aid and discontinue military sales (Wiegand 1969). It also orchestrated a military coup in Ecuador, which removed from office Carlos Julio Arosemena, a President determined to enforce the 200 nm claim, and thus managed to secure a temporary exemption for US fishing vessels from the new military government (Pineo 207:172–176). Yet, the Court could not ignore that the claim had established a seaward boundary, even though, for the purpose of determining the extent of the lateral boundary it assumed that the 200 nm claim was irrelevant. This boundary, though not universally recognised, was strongly enforced and respected by most countries in the region.

Ultimately, the Court faced the dilemma of reconciling its decision to ignore the 200 nm claim, in order to justify its finding on the extent of the lateral boundary, with the widespread practice, which indicated that the claim was widely recognized in the region and effectively enforced by the claimants. As ever, Judge Owada anticipated this dilemma and proposed a solution. He argued that there were two boundaries: a de facto lateral boundary with a seaward extension of 80 nm; and an external horizontal 200 nm boundary established by the *Santiago Declaration* and designed to prevent distant fishing vessels from exploiting the resources in the maritime zone (Owada #26(2)). The Court did not explicitly accept Judge Owada's two-boundary solution, but did so implicitly. It held that, although the parties had failed explicitly to delimit their lateral boundary they had, nonetheless, established and enforced a seaward maritime boundary of 200 nm to exclude distant fishing fleets (#127). The implication of the Court's reasoning was that there were two boundaries: one, with a seaward extension of 200 nm, enforced by the parties and respected by third states; and, the other, a tacitly agreed lateral boundary, which only had a seaward extension of 80 nm. This two-boundary solution is implausible. It assumes that beyond the 80 nm point there was no lateral boundary and that for more than fifty years the parties had not noticed that more than half of the area claimed under the *Santiago Declaration* had not been delimited. This disjointed boundary arrangement highlights, yet again, the absurd consequences created by the Court's erroneous inference that the parties had concluded a tacit agreement.

D. Final remarks

These remarks address two questions arising from the materials discussed in Part II: the question of evidence and the question of equity.

1. Evidence

The information on which the Court relied to determine the extent of the lateral boundary was limited and inadequate. It was incidental information supplied by the parties on their fishing activities and was not intended to assist the Court in determining the seaward extent of the lateral boundary. Judge Donoghue noted this point, but did not believe it had prevented the Court from arriving at a sound outcome (Donoghue Declaration). Whether the outcome was sound is, of course, a matter of opinion. What is interesting, however, is to consider why, despite its broad fact-finding powers, the Court did not ask the parties to produce additional evidence, or why it did not appoint experts to investigate the practice of the parties in the vicinity of the boundary. Article 49 of the Court's Statute allows the Court—'even before the hearings begin'—to request the parties to produce documents or to provide explanations. Article 50 allows the Court 'at any time' to appoint an individual or an institution to carry out an 'enquiry' or to give an expert opinion. The Court, however, has rarely used these powers (for recent detailed studies on these points, see Devaney 2016:14–27, 73–126; Weisburd 2015:189–221). Since in this case the finding that the parties had entered into a tacit agreement was a legal inference not based on facts, it is hardly surprising that the Court did not use its fact-finding powers. Furthermore, a proper inquiry into the activities of the parties in the vicinity of the boundary would have had to include whale hunting. Since the Court had dismissed this activity as irrelevant, on the ground that it had not been included in the FAO statistics, a proper inquiry into the activities of the parties would have made it impossible for the Court to ignore the 200 nm claim.

2. Equity

Peru argued, successfully, that Paragraph IV of the *Santiago Declaration* only applied to the maritime zones of islands where their maritime zones overlapped with the maritime zone generated by the continent. It also argued, eloquently and consistently, that due to the slightly concave nature of the parties' coast it was inconceivable that in 1952 Peru would have accepted the parallel of latitude as a method of delimitation, since it would have drastically reduced its maritime entitlement (PR:274, 281). Chile insisted that the question before the Court was not whether the outcome was equitable, but whether in 1952 the parties had agreed to delimit their lateral boundary. It also noted that equity demanded that the parties respect their agreed boundary (CR:7).

The Court did not address Peru's argument about equity. Yet, it cannot be ignored that the tacit agreement gave each party half of what they claimed. Peru obtained nearly half of the 35,000 square kilometres it had claimed, while Chile retained important fishing grounds within 80 nm off its coast. This outcome might suggest that the Court was determined to split the difference, thus avoiding an outcome that the parties might have rejected. Had the Court been authorised by the parties to decide the case *ex aequo et bono*, it is likely that the result would have been similar. The parties, however, gave the Court jurisdiction to rule in accordance with international law. They did not authorise the Court to enter a judgment based upon 'an exercise of discretion or conciliation' or to engage 'in an operation of distributive justice' (*Continental Shelf (Tunisia/Libyan Arab Jamahiriya)*, Judgment, I.C.J. Reports 1982, 18 at 60).

It could well be argued that the Court, perhaps inadvertently, combined the rules on treaty interpretation with the rules on the delimitation of the continental shelf and the EEZ between states with adjacent coasts. These rules, UNCLOS Articles 74 and 83, provide that delimitation 'shall be effected by agreement on the basis of international law, as referred to in Article 38 of the Statute of the International Court of Justice, in order to achieve an equitable solution'. The view that the rules on maritime delimitation might have influenced the outcome of this case is, of course, speculative. Nevertheless, had this been the case, it might explain why the tacit agreement designed by the Court divides the disputed area almost equally between the parties.

Conclusion

This book focuses on two issues: the interpretation of the *Santiago Declaration* and its connected treaties; and the tacit agreement that established a lateral maritime boundary with a seaward extension of 80 nm. Part I argues that the Court's finding that the *Santiago Declaration* did not delimit the lateral boundary is mistaken because it ignores its context, as well as its object and purpose. Part II argues that the finding that the parties had entered into a tacit agreement is an unjustified legal inference derived from a hasty interpretation of the *Special Agreement* of 1954. It questions the reliability of the evidence used to determine the seaward extent of the lateral boundary and argues that the Court failed to demonstrate the bearing of contemporaneous developments in the law of the sea on the content of the tacit agreement.

The Court's Judgment combines an unrestrained textual approach to interpretation with a remarkable disregard for the comprehensive legal framework established by the parties to govern and manage their maritime claim. These two features are closely linked, which explains the inconsistencies of the Court's reasoning. Consistency is, of course, not a criterion of truth, but inconsistency often conceals errors.

The Court observes that the *Santiago Declaration* is not a delimitation treaty because it lacks the standard features of such treaties. Yet, it finds that Paragraph IV of the *Declaration* delimits the maritime zone of islands if they overlap with the maritime zone of a neighbouring country. This finding suggests that the parties were not constrained by contemporaneous principles of international law; they simply chose not to delimit their entire boundary. The Court does not deny that the parties could have defined their entire boundary had they so wished. Yet, when it concludes, mistakenly in my view, that the phrase 'maritime boundary' in the *Special Agreement* indicates that the parties had entered into a tacit agreement, it does not even contemplate the possibility that the special zone established by this Agreement could have had an extension of 200 nm, even though, during the litigation, the parties assumed it did. Had the Court accepted that the seaward extension of the special zone was 200 nm, Chile's argument would have prevailed. The Court, however, did not follow this path. As a consequence, it had to give content to the tacit agreement. This was not an easy task as the Court had to overcome three obstacles: the status of the celebrated 200 nm claim, the longstanding practice of the parties and the elaborate legal framework established by the parties to manage their claim.

The Court could not easily ignore the 200 nm claim as this was the most distinctive feature of the entire case. Indeed, the finding that the boundary was an all-purpose boundary was based upon three documents that were primarily concerned with the 200 nm claim: the *Santiago Declaration* and the parties' respective unilateral declarations of 1947. The Court, however, resolved the problem of the 200 nm claim creatively: it made it disappear. It characterised the claim as a policy aspiration designed to achieve international solidarity, thus denying that it had any legal force. By transforming the 200 nm claim into a policy aspiration the Court could justify its finding that the lateral boundary had a seaward extension that was less than half of the extent claimed by the parties. The curious reference to the parties' limited extractive capacity was also part of the effort to minimise the significance of the 200 nm claim. The Court, however, could not ignore the claim altogether. Indeed it did acknowledge that on several occasions the parties had enforced their claim well beyond 80 nm, as was the case in 1954 when Peru seized the Onassis whaling fleet. This ambivalence led the Court to suggest, albeit implicitly, that there were two boundaries: a lateral boundary with a seaward extension of 80 nm and an external boundary of 200 nm designed to keep distant fishing fleets out of their respective maritime zones.

The practice of the parties did not present a major challenge for the Court. Since the Court concluded that Paragraph IV of the *Declaration* applied only to the lateral boundary of islands, and, as there are no islands in the vicinity of the Chile/Peru boundary, the implication was that Paragraph IV does not apply to Chile. The Court regarded this finding as irrefutable and declined to consider any evidence to the contrary. It did not even pause to consider whether the reference to the maritime boundary in the *Special Agreement* was at odds with its interpretation of the *Santiago Declaration*. The Court acknowledged, however, that the practice of the parties did have a bearing on the determination of the extent of the lateral boundary. The parties, however, did not submit any evidence that was directly relevant to this point. This is unsurprising since the Court's finding was unexpected, and both Chile and Peru had explicitly rejected the possibility that the boundary could have been established by tacit agreement. As a result, the Court confined its inquiry on the extent of the lateral boundary to the parties' fishing activities, while conveniently excluding whale hunting. Since the evidence submitted by the parties on their fishing activities was limited and not intended to determine the seaward extent of the boundary, the Court's findings are unconvincing. Its view that fishing was carried out by small vessels within 60 to 80 nm from the coast is pure speculation since it does not specify the size of these vessels. It is also unpersuasive because the *Special Agreement* had established a special zone for small vessels, thus implying that larger vessels also operated in the area.

The elaborate legal framework established by the parties to manage various aspects of their claim was also an obstacle for the Court. The legal instruments comprising this framework presupposed that the signatories to the *Santiago Declaration* had separate well-defined maritime zones. The legal status of six of these agreements, concluded in Lima in 1954, was especially important because they all included the same standard clause providing that they were an integral and supplementary part of the agreements and resolutions adopted in Santiago in 1952. This clause had the effect of transforming the Lima Agreements into context for the purpose of the interpretation of the *Santiago Declaration*. The Court, however, dismissed this clause on the ground that it was introduced late during the drafting process. After dismissing the critical connection between the *Santiago Declaration* and the Lima Agreements, the Court set aside the parties' comprehensive legal framework with relative ease. First, it examined only some of the Lima Agreements and only with the purpose of ascertaining whether any of their clauses delimited the lateral boundary. And second, it rejected the argument that these instruments presupposed that the parties had separate maritime zones on the ground that the zones mentioned in these instruments were the outcome of an initial allocation. The Court offered no support for this statement and said nothing about what might have happened after the so-called initial allocation. In the end, the Court regarded the elaborate legal framework established by the parties between 1952 and 1954 as a variety of soft law, which, as such, did not have to be taken seriously.

The Court also sought support from international law to determine the extent of the lateral boundary. Although it links its finding on the extent of the lateral boundary to the practice of other states and the work of the International Law Commission, it does not state whether international law would have prevented the parties from tacitly agreeing to a boundary beyond 80 nm. Instead, it relies on the parties' response to a question from the Bench to suggest that the 200 nm claim was not enforceable. The question from the Bench appeared to assume that under contemporaneous international law the only maritime claims that were enforceable were those with a maximum seaward extension of 12 nm. Under this standard, neither the 80 nm lateral boundary established by the Court nor the parties' 200 nm claim would have been enforceable. This explains why the Court refrained from explicitly stating that the 200 nm claim was unenforceable. Indeed, as the materials in Part II show, contemporaneous international law did not prevent the parties from establishing, *inter se*, a lateral boundary extending well beyond 80 nm.

In any event, it is not easy to discern the objective of the Court's inquiry into contemporary developments in the law of the sea. Given that the undisputed intention of the parties in 1952 was to challenge prevailing practices on the breadth of the territorial sea, it is unlikely that they would have tacitly agreed to a lateral boundary less extensive than their 200 nm claim. The notion that the parties had suddenly become compliant with contemporary principles of the law of the sea is absurd. It is inconsistent with the ten agreements they concluded between 1952 and 1954. It is also inconsistent with their practice, public statements and, especially, their active participation at three Law of the Sea Conferences between 1958 and 1982.

Strict textual interpretation is often favoured because it is seen as a safeguard against excessive judicial discretion. The Judgment in this case does not support this view. For in this case a strictly textual approach, devoid of context and oblivious of the purposes sought by the parties, provided the Court with a platform to design an agreement that had no basis in the parties' longstanding practice and could only be justified by ignoring their comprehensive legal framework. This book has shown that strict adherence to a textual method of interpretation does not guarantee either judicial self-restraint or an equitable outcome in accordance with the law.

Annex 1

Declaration on the Maritime Zone*

1   Governments have the obligation to ensure for their peoples the necessary conditions of subsistence, and to provide them with the resources for their economic development.

2   Consequently, they are responsible for the conservation and protection of their natural resources and for the regulation of the development of these resources in order to secure the best possible advantages for their respective countries.

3   Thus, it is also their duty to prevent any exploitation of these resources, beyond the scope of their jurisdiction, which endangers the existence, integrity and conservation of these resources to the detriment of the peoples who, because of their geographical situation, possess irreplaceable means of subsistence and vital economic resources in their seas.

In view of the foregoing considerations, the Governments of Chile, Ecuador and Peru, determined to conserve and safeguard for their respective peoples the natural resources of the maritime zones adjacent to their coasts, formulate the following Declaration:

I   The geological and biological factors which determine the existence, conservation and development of marine fauna and flora in the waters along the coasts of the countries making the Declaration are such that the former extension of the territorial sea and the contiguous zone are inadequate for the purposes of the conservation, development and exploitation of these resources, to which the coastal countries are entitled.

II   In the light of these circumstances, the Governments of Chile, Ecuador and Peru proclaim as a norm of their international

* United Nations Treaty Series, Registration Number 14758

maritime policy that they each possess exclusive sovereignty and jurisdiction over the sea along the coasts of their respective countries to a minimum distance of 200 nautical miles from these coasts.

III The exclusive jurisdiction and sovereignty over this maritime zone shall also encompass exclusive sovereignty and jurisdiction over the seabed and the subsoil thereof.

IV In the case of island territories, the zone of 200 nautical miles shall apply to the entire coast of the island or group of islands. If an island or group of islands belonging to one of the countries making the declaration is situated less than 200 nautical miles from the general maritime zone belonging to another of those countries, the maritime zone of the island or group of islands shall be limited by the parallel at the point at which the land frontier of the States concerned reaches the sea.

V This declaration shall be without prejudice to the necessary limitations to the exercise of sovereignty and jurisdiction established under international law to allow innocent and inoffensive passage through the area indicated for ships of all nations.

VI For the application of the principles contained in this Declaration, the Governments of Chile, Ecuador and Peru hereby announce their intention to sign agreements or conventions which shall establish general norms to regulate and protect hunting and fishing within the maritime zone belonging to them, and to regulate and coordinate the exploitation and development of all other kinds of products or natural resources existing in these waters which are of common interest.

Santiago 18 August 1952

Annex 2

Complementary Convention to the Declaration of Sovereignty over the Maritime Zone of Two Hundred Miles*

The Governments of the Republics of Chile, Ecuador and Peru, in conformity with the provisions of resolution X of 8 October 1954, signed
at Santiago de Chile by the Standing Committee of the Conference on
the Exploitation and Conservation of' the Maritime Resources of the
South Pacific,

Having noted be proposals and recommendations approved in
October of this year by the said Standing Committee,

Have appointed the following plenipotentiaries....

And Whereas...

Chile, Ecuador and Peru have proclaimed their sovereignty over the
sea adjacent to the coasts of their respective countries to a distance of
not less than two hundred nautical miles from the said coasts the seabed and the subsoil of this maritime zone being included.

The Government of Chile, Ecuador and Peru, at the First Conference on the Exploitation and Conservation of the Maritime Resources
of the South Pacific, held at Santiago de Chile in 1952, expressed their
intention of entering into agreements or conventions relating to the
application of the principles governing that sovereignty, for the purpose in particular of' regulating and protecting hunting and fisheries
within their several maritime zones:

Now Therefore the Said Plenipotentiaries Hereby Agree as Follows:

1   Chile, Ecuador and Peru shall consult with one another for the
    purpose of upholding, in law, the principle of their sovereignty
    over the maritime zone to a distance of not less than two hundred
    nautical miles, including the sea-bed and the subsoil correspond-
    ing thereto. The term "nautical mile" means the equivalent of
    one minute of the arc measured on the Equator, or a distance of
    1,852.8 meters.

* *Revista Peruana de Derecho Internacional*, Number 46, 1954, pp. 276ff.

2   If any complaints or protests should be addressed to any of the Parties, or if proceedings should be instituted against a Party in a court of law or in an arbitral tribunal, whether possessing general or special jurisdiction, the contracting countries undertake to consult with one another concerning the case to be presented for the defence and furthermore bind themselves to co-operate fully with one another in the joint defence.

3   In the event of a violation of the said maritime zone by force, the State affected shall report the event immediately to the other Contracting Parties, for the purpose of determining what action should be taken to safeguard the sovereignty which has been violated.

4   Each of' the Contracting Parties undertakes not to enter into any agreements, arrangements or conventions which imply a diminution of the sovereignty over the said zone, though this provision shall not prejudice their rights to enter into agreements or to conclude contracts which do not conflict with the common rules laid down by the contracting countries.

5   All the provisions of this Agreement shall be deemed to be an integral and supplementary part of, and not in any way to abrogate, the resolutions and decisions adopted at the Conference on the Exploitation and Conservation of the Maritime Resources of the South Pacific, held at Santiago de Chile in August 1952.

Lima 4 December 1954

Annex 3

Agreement Relating to a Special Maritime Frontier Zone*

The Governments of the Republics of Chile, Ecuador and Peru, in conformity with the provisions of Resolution X of 8 October 1954, signed at Santiago de Chile by the Standing Committee of the Conference on the Exploitation and Conservation of the Maritime Resources of the South Pacific,

Having noted the proposals and recommendations approved in October of this year by the said Standing Committee,

Have appointed as their Plenipotentiaries …. who,

Considering that:

Experience has shown that innocent and inadvertent violations of the maritime frontier between adjacent States occur frequently because small vessels manned by crews with insufficient knowledge of navigation or not equipped with the necessary instruments have difficulty in determining accurately their position on the high seas;

The application of penalties in such cases always produces ill-feeling in the fishermen and friction between the countries concerned, which may affect adversely the spirit of cooperation and unity which should at all times prevail among the countries signatories to the instruments signed at Santiago; and

It is desirable to avoid the occurrence of such unintentional infringements, the consequences of which affect principally the fishermen;

Have agreed as follows:

1   A special zone is hereby established, at a distance of 12 nautical miles from the coast, extending to a breadth of 10 nautical miles on either side of the parallel which constitutes a maritime boundary between the two countries.

---

* United Nations Treaty Series, Registration Number 40521.

2   The accidental presence in the said zone of a vessel of either of the adjacent countries, which is a vessel of the name described in the paragraph beginning with the words "Experience has shown" in the preamble hereto, shall not be considered to be a violation of the waters of the maritime zone, though this provision shall not be construed as recognizing any right to engage, with deliberate intent, in hunting or fishing in the said special zone.

3   Fishing or hunting within the zone of 12 nautical miles from the coast shall be reserved exclusively to the nationals of each country.

4   All the provisions of this Agreement shall be deemed to be an integral and supplementary part of, and not in any way to abrogate, the resolutions and decisions adopted at the Conference on the Exploitation and Conservation of the Maritime Resources of the South Pacific, held in Santiago de Chile in August 1952.

Lima 4 December 1954

Annex 4
Agreements between Chile, Ecuador and Peru concluded in 1952 and 1954*

1952: Santiago 18 August 1952

Declaration on the Maritime Zone (Santiago Declaration)
(Declaración de Santiago, Declaración sobre Zona Marítima)

Agreement on the Organization of the Standing Committee on the Use and Conservation of the Marine Resources of the South Pacific
(Convenio sobre Organización de la Comisión Permanente de la Conferencia sobre Explotación y Conservación de las Riquezas Marítimas del Pacífico Sur)

Joint Declaration on Fishery Problems in the South Pacific
(Declaración Conjunta relativa a los Problemas de la Pesquería en el Pacífico Sur)

Regulations Governing Whaling in the Waters of the South Pacific (Whale Hunting Regulation)
(Reglamento para las Faenas de Caza Marítima en las Aguas del Pacífico Sur) (Reglamento para caza de ballenas)

1954: Lima 4 December 1954

Complementary Convention to the Declaration of Sovereignty over the Maritime Zone of Two Hundred Miles
(Convenio Complementario a la Declaración de Soberanía sobre la Zona Marítima de 200 Millas)

Convention on the System of Sanctions
(Convenio sobre Sistema de Sanciones)

---

* Spanish text in Comisión Permanente del Pacífico Sur 2007:5–8, 59–82, English translation in US Naval War College 1956:264–289.

Convention on Measures of Surveillance and Control in the Maritime Zones of the Signatory Countries
(Convenio sobre Medidas de Vigilancia y Control de las Zonas Marítimas de los Países Signatarios)

Convention on the Granting of Permits for the Exploitation of the Resources of the South Pacific
(Convenio sobre Otorgamiento de Permisos para la Explotación de las Riquezas del Pacífico Sur)

Convention on the Ordinary Annual Meeting of the Permanent Commission for the South Pacific (for whaling activities)
(Convenio sobre la Reunión Ordinaria Anual de la Comisión Permanente del Pacífico Sur) (Para actividades de caza de ballenas)

Agreement relating to a Special Maritime Frontier Zone
(Convenio sobre Zona Especial Fronteriza Marítima)

References

Cases

Acquisition of Polish Nationality, Advisory Opinion, 1923, P.C. I. J., Series B, No. 7, 20.

Ambatielos case (Greece v. United Kingdom), (Jurisdiction), I.C.J. Reports, 1952, 28.

Conditions of Admission of a State to Membership in the United Nations (Article 4 of the Charter (Advisory Opinion), I.C.J. Reports 1948, 57.

Continental Shelf (Tunisia/Libyan Arab Jamahiriya), Judgment, I.C.J. Reports 1982, 18.

Diversion of Water from the River Meuse (Netherlands v. Belgium), Judgment, 1937, P.C.I.J., Series A/B, No. 70, 4 (paragraph 34).

Fisheries case (United Kingdom v. Norway), Judgment, I.C.J. Reports 1951, 116.

Fisheries Jurisdiction (Federal Republic of Germany v. Iceland), Merits, Judgment, I.C.J. Reports 1974, 175.

Fisheries Jurisdiction (United Kingdom v. Iceland), Merits, Judgment, I.C.J. Reports 1974, 3.

Maritime Delimitation and Territorial Questions between Qatar and Bahrain, Merits, Judgment, I.C.J. Reports 2001, 40.

Maritime Delimitation in the Black Sea (Romania v. Ukraine), Judgment, I.C.J. Reports 2009, 61.

Maritime Dispute (Peru v. Chile), Judgment, I.C.J. Reports 2014, 3.

North Sea Continental Shelf, Judgment, I.C.J. Reports 1969, 3.

Sovereignty over Pedra Branca/Pulau Batu Puteh, Middle Rocks and South Ledge (Malaysia/Singapore), Judgment, I.C.J. Reports 2008, 12.

Territorial and Maritime Dispute between Nicaragua and Honduras in the Caribbean Sea (Nicaragua v. Honduras), Judgment, I.C.J. Reports 2007, 659.

Territorial Dispute Libyan Jamahirija/Chad, Judgment, I.C.J. Reports 1994, 6.

Official documents

Second United Nations Conference on the Law of the Sea, 1960, Official Records, Summary Records of Plenary Meetings and of Meetings of the Committee of the Whole.

Third United Nations Conference on the Law of the Sea, 1973–1982, Vol. XVI, Eleventh Session.

United Nations Conference on the Law of Treaties, Official Records, 1968 (First Session, 26 March to 27 May).

United Nations Conference on the Law of the Sea 1958, Volume I.

United Nations Conference on the Law of the Sea 1958, Volume III.

United Nations Conference on the Law of the Sea 1958, Volume IV.

United Nations Conference on the Law of the Sea 1958, Volume VI.

Yearbook of the International Law Commission, 1956, Vol. I.

Yearbook of the International Law Commission, 1956, Vol. II.

Yearbook of the International Law Commission, 1964, Vol. II.

Yearbook of the International Law Commission, 1966, Vol. I.

Minutes

Minutes of the First Session of the Legal Affairs Commission of the First Conference on the Exploitation and Conservation of Marine Resources of the South Pacific, 11 August 1952, PM Annex 56.

Minutes of the Second Session of the Legal Affairs Commission of the First Conference on the Exploitation and Conservation of Marine Resources of the South Pacific, 12 August 1952, CCM Annex 34.

Minutes of the First Session of Commission I of the Second Conference on the Exploitation and Conservation of Marine Resources of the South Pacific, 2 December 1954, CCM Annex 38.

Minutes of the Second Session of Commission I of the Second Conference on the Exploitation and Conservation of Marine Resources of the South Pacific, 3 December 1954, CCM Annex 39.

Final Minutes of the Second Conference on Conservation and Exploitation of the Marine Resources of the South Pacific, 3 December 1954, CCM: Annex No. 40.

Books and articles in journals

Abugattás, Gattas (2014), 'Análisis sobre la Referencia a los Acuerdos Tácitos en algunos Casos de Delimitación Marítima, con Especial Atención al Asunto de la Delimitación Marítima entre Perú y Chile', *Agenda Internacional*, Vol. 21 (32), pp. 79–105.

Aguayo, Francisca (2014), 'Reflexiones sobre el Derecho Internacional y la Delimitación Marítima', *Revista Tribuna Internacional*, Vol. 3 (5), pp. 87–102.

Aramburu y Menchaca, Andrés A. (1953), 'Character and Scope of the Rights Declared and Practiced over the Continental Sea and Shelf', *American Journal of International Law*, Vol. 47, pp. 120–123.

Arnello Romo, Mario (2014), 'La Sentencia de la Corte Internacional de Justicia sobre el Límite Marítimo entre Perú y Chile', *Revista Tribuna Internacional*, Vol. 3 (Número Especial), pp. 61–69.

Aust, Anthony (2000), *Modern Treaty Law and Practice*, Cambridge: Cambridge University Press.

Baxter, Richard (1956), 'The Territorial Sea', *American Society of International Law Proceedings*, Vol. 50, pp. 116–124.

Bayitch, S.A. (1956), 'International Fishery Problems in the Western Hemisphere', *Miami Law Quarterly*, Vol. 10, pp. 499–506.

Beckett, Eric (1950), 'The Interpretation of Treaties', *Annuaire de l'Institut de Droit International*, Vol. 43, pp. 435–444.

Bingham, Joseph Walter (1938), *Report on the International Law of Pacific Coast Fisheries*, Stanford: Stanford University Press.

Bingham, Joseph Walter (1940), 'Changing Concepts of International Law: Maritime Jurisdiction in Time of Peace', *American Society of International Law Proceedings*, Vol. 34, pp. 54–63.

Bishop, William J. (1962), 'The 1958 Convention on Fishing and Conservation of the Living Resources of the High Seas', *Columbia Law Review*, Vol. 62, pp. 1206–1229.

Boggs, S. Whittemore (1951), 'National Claims in Adjacent Seas', *Geographical Review*, Vol. 41 (2), pp. 185–209.

Borchard, Edwin (1946), 'The Resources of the Continental Shelf', *American Journal of International Law*, Vol. 40 (1), pp. 53–70.

Bowett, D.W. (1960), 'The Second United Nations Conference on the Law of the Sea', *International and Comparative Law Quarterly*, Vol. 9, pp. 415–435.

Brierly, J.L. (1963), *The Law of Nations*, (sixth edition), Oxford: Oxford University Press.

Brunnée, Jutta (2012), 'Treaty Amendments', in Duncan Hollis (ed.), *The Oxford Guide to Treaties*, Oxford: Oxford University Press, pp. 346–366.

Churchill, Robin (2015), 'Dispute Settlement in the Law of the Sea: Survey for 2014', *International Journal of Marine and Coastal Law*, Vol. 30, pp. 585–653.

Churchill, Robin R. and Geir Ulfstein (2000), 'Autonomous Institutional Arrangements in Multilateral Environmental Agreements: A Little Noticed Phenomenon in International Law', *American Journal of International Law*, Vol. 94, pp. 623–659.

Comisión Permanente del Pacífico Sur (2007), *Convenios, Acuerdos, Protocolos, Declaraciones, Estatuto y Reglamento de la Comisión Permanente del Pacífico Sur*, Quito, Ecuador.

Dean, Arthur H. (1960), 'The Second Geneva Conference on the Law of the Sea: The Fight for Freedom of the Seas', *American Journal of International Law*, Vol. 54 (4), pp. 751–789.

Devaney, James Gerard (2016), *Fact-finding before the International Court of Justice*, Cambridge: Cambridge University Press.

Dorr, Oliver (2012), 'Interpretation of Treaties', in Oliver Dorr and Kirsten Schmalenbach (eds.), *Vienna Convention on the Law of Treaties: A Commentary*, Heidelberg: Springer, pp. 521–604.

Doucet, W.F. and H. Einarsson (1966), 'A Brief Description of Peruvian Fisheries', *California Cooperative Oceanic Fisheries Investigations, Reports*, Volume 11, 1 July 1963 to 30 June 1966, pp. 82–87.

Eckert, Ross D. (1979), *The Enclosure of Ocean Resources*, Stanford University: Hoover Institution.

Evans, Malcolm D. (2015), 'Maritime Delimitation', in Donald R. Rothwell, Alex G. Oude Elferink, Karen N. Scott, Tim Stephens (eds.), *The Oxford Handbook of the Law of the Sea*, Oxford: Oxford University Press, pp. 254–279.

Evensen, Jens (1952), 'The Anglo-Norwegian Fisheries Case and Its Legal Consequences', *American Journal of International Law*, Vol. 46 (4), pp. 609–630.

Ferrero, Eduardo (1974), 'Fundamento de la Soberanía Marítima del Perú hasta las 200 millas', *Derecho: Revista de la Facultad de Derecho, Pontficia Universidad Católica del Peru*, Vol. 32, pp. 38–61.

Fiedler, Reginald H. (1944), 'The Peruvian Fisheries', *Geographical Review*, Vol. 34 (1), pp. 96–119.

Finley, Carmel (2009), 'The Social Construction of Fishing', *Ecology and Society*, Vol. 14 (1), p. 6 [online] www.ecologyandsociety.org/vol14/iss1/art6/.

Finley, Carmel and Naomi Oreskes (2013), 'Food for Thought: Maximum Sustained Yield, a Policy Disguised as Science', *ICES Journal of Marine Science*, Vol. 70 (2), pp. 245–255.

Fish, Stanley (2005), 'There Is No Textualist Position', *San Diego Law Review*, Vol. 42, pp. 629–650.

Fitzmaurice, Gerald (1951), 'The Law and Procedure of the International Court of Justice, 1951–4: Treaty Interpretation and Certain Other Treaty Points', *British Yearbook of International Law*, Vol. 28, pp. 1–28.

Fitzmaurice, Gerald (1957), 'The Law and Procedure of the International Court of Justice, 1951–4: Treaty Interpretation and Other Treaty Points', *British Yearbook of International Law*, Vol. 33, pp. 203–293.

Fitzmaurice, Gerald (1963), 'Hersch Lauterpacht—The Scholar as a Judge, Part III', *British Yearbook of International Law*, Vol. 37, pp. 133–188.

Fitzmaurice, Malgosia A. (1997), 'Modifications to the Principles of Consent in Relation to Certain Treaty Obligations', *Austrian Review of International & European Law*, Vol. 2, pp. 275–317.

Fitzmaurice, Malgosia A. (2005), 'Consent to Be Bound—Anything New under the Sun?', *Nordic Journal of International Law*, Vol. 14, pp. 483–508.

Fleischer, Carl August (1988), 'The New Regime of Maritime Fisheries', *Collected Courses of the Hague Academy of International Law*, Vol. 209, pp. 96–222.

Flores, Ramiro Alberto (2011), 'Los Balleneros Anglo-Estadunidenses y la Cuestión de la "Extranjerización" del Comercio Peruano a Fines de la Época Colonial, 1790–1820', *America Latina en La Historia Económica*, No. 36, pp. 39–64.

Francois, J.P.A. (1955), 'Some Aspects of the Extension of National Sovereignty to the Adjacent Sea', *International Relations*, Vol. 1 (3), pp. 79–83.

García-Amador, F.V. (1974), 'The Latin American Contribution to the Development of the Law of the Sea', *American Journal of International Law*, Vol. 68, pp. 33–50.

García-Sayan, Enrique (1974), 'La Doctrina de las 200 Millas y el Derecho del Mar', *Derecho: Revista de la Facultad de Derecho, Pontficia Universidad Católica del Peru*, Vol. 32, pp. 12–27.

Gardiner, Richard (2008), *Treaty Interpretation*, Oxford: Oxford University Press.

Gidel, Gilbert (1934), 'La Mer Territoriale et la Zone Contigue', *Collected Courses of the Hague Academy of International Law*, Vol. 48, pp. 137–278.

Glantz, Michael H. (1979), 'Science, Politics and Economics of the Peruvian Anchoveta Fishery', *Marine Policy* (July), Vol. 3 (3), pp. 201–210.

Goldie, L.F.E. (1969), 'The Ocean's Resources and International Law', *Columbia Journal of Transnational Law*, Vol. 8, pp. 1–53.

Grafton, R. Quentin, Ray Hilborn, Dale Squires and Meryl J. Williams (2010), 'Marine Conservation and Fisheries Management: At the Crossroads', in R. Quentin Grafton et al. (eds.), *Handbook of Marine Fisheries Conservation and Management*, New York: Oxford University Press, pp. 3–19.

Graham, Kimberley (2015), 'Ocean Order in South America: The Maritime Dispute between Peru and Chile', *International Journal of Marine and Coastal Law*, Vol. 30, pp. 361–370.

Gray, Christine (2015), 'The 2014 Judicial Activity of the International Court of Justice', *American Journal of International Law*, Vol. 109 (3), pp. 583–609.

Gros, André (1959), "La Convention sur la Pêche et la Conservation des Ressources Biologiques de la Haute Mer', *Collected Courses of the Hague Academy of International Law*, Vol. 97, pp. 5–88.

Hollick, Ann L. (1976–1977), 'U.S. Oceans Policy: The Truman Proclamations', *Virginia Journal of International Law*, Vol. 17, pp. 23–55.

Hollick, Ann L. (1977), 'The Origins of 200-Mile Offshore Zones', *American Journal of International Law*, Vol. 71 (3), pp. 494–500.

Hollick, Ann L. (1978), 'The Roots of US Fisheries Policy', *Ocean Development and International Law*, Vol. 5, pp. 61–105.

Horna, Hernán (1968), 'The Fish Industry of Peru', *Journal of Developing Areas*, Vol. 2 (3), pp. 393–406.

Hyde, Charles Cheney (1909), 'Treaty Interpretation', *American Journal of International Law*, Vol. 3, (1), pp. 46–61.

Infante, María Teresa (2014), 'Peru v. Chile: The International Court of Justice Decides on the Status of the Maritime Boundary', *Chinese Journal of International Law*, Vol. 13, pp. 741–762.

Jagota, S.P. (1981), 'Maritime Boundary', *Collected Courses of The Hague Academy of International Law*, Vol. 171, pp. 85–220.

Jennings, R. and A. Watts, eds. (1992), *Oppenheim's International Law, Vol. 1: Peace, Parts 2 to 4*, (ninth edition), London: Longmans.

Jennings, Robert Y. (1997), 'The Role of the International Court of Justice', *British Yearbook of International Law*, Vol. 68, pp. 1–63.

Jessup, Philip C. (1947), 'Modernization of the Law of International Contractual Arrangements', *American Journal of International Law*, Vol. 41, pp. 378–405.

Jessup, Philip C. (1955), 'The International Law Commission's 1954 Report on the Regime of the Territorial Sea', *American Journal of International Law*, Vol. 49 (2), pp. 221–229.

Jiménez de Aréchaga, Eduardo (1993), 'Chile-Peru (1952), Report Number 3–5', in Jonathan I. Charney and Lewis M. Alexander (eds.), *International Maritime Boundaries*, Leiden: Brill-Nijhoff, pp. 793–800.

Kraska, James (2011), *Maritime Power and the Law of the Sea*, Oxford: Oxford University Press.

Krueger Robert B. and Myron H. Nordquist (1979), 'The Evolution of the 200-Mile Exclusive Economic Zone: State Practice in the Pacific Basin', *Virginia Journal of International Law,* Vol. 19, pp. 321–400.

Kunz, Josef L. (1956), 'Continental Shelf and International Law: Confusion and Abuse', *American Journal of International Law*, Vol. 50 (4), pp. 828–853.

Lauterpacht, Hersch (1949), 'Restrictive Interpretation and the Principle of Effectiveness in the Interpretation of Treaties', *British Year Book of International Law*, Vol. 26, pp. 48–85.

Lauterpacht, Hersch (1955), 'Codification and Development of International Law', *American Journal of International Law*, Vol. 49 (1), pp. 16–43.

Linderfalk, Ulf (2007), *On the Interpretation of Treaties*, Dordrecht, The Netherlands: Springer.

Lopez Escarcena, Sebastián (2014), 'La disputa marítima entre Perú y Chile', *Revista Chilena de Derecho*, Vol. 13 (3), pp. 1133–1153.

Loring, David C. (1971), 'The United States-Peruvian "Fisheries" Dispute', *Stanford Law Review*, Vol. 23 (3), pp. 391–453.

Lux, William R. (1971), 'The Peruvian Fishing Industry: A Case Study in Capitalism at Work', *Revista de Historia de America*, Vol. 71, pp. 137–146.

Magnuson, Warren G. (1977), 'The Fishery Conservation and Management Act of 1976: First Step toward Improved Management of Marine Fisheries', *Washington Law Review*, Vol. 52, pp. 427–450.

Martens, Ernst K. (1976), 'Evolution of the Coastal State Jurisdiction: A Conflict between Developed and Developing Nations', *Ecology Law Quarterly*, Vol. 5 (3), pp. 531–553.

Matz-Lück, Nele and Johannes Fuchs (2015), 'Marine Living Resources', in Donald Rothwell, Alex Oude Elferink, Karen Scott, and Tim Stephens (eds.), *Oxford Handbook of the Law of the Sea*, Oxford: Oxford University Press, pp. 491–515.

Meron, Theodor (1975), 'The Fishermen's Protective Act: A Case Study in Contemporary Legal Strategy of the United States', *American Journal of International Law*, Vol. 69 (2), pp. 290–309.

Meyer, Charles A. (1972), 'Department Reviews Fisheries Disputes and Their Effect on Inter-American Relations', *Department of State Bulletin*, Vol. 66 (1705), pp. 284–287.

Novak, Fabián and Luis García-Corrochano (2014), 'Presentación y Análisis General del Fallo de la Corte Internacional de Justicia de La Haya sobre el Diferendo Marítimo entre el Perú y Chile', *Agenda Internacional*, Vol. 21 (32), pp. 23–49.

Oda, Shigeru (1955), 'The Territorial Sea and Natural Resources', *International and Comparative Law Quarterly*, Vol. 4 (3), pp. 415–425.

Orrego, Francisco (1999), *The Changing International Law of High Sea Fisheries*, Cambridge: Cambridge University Press.

Oxman, Bernard H. (1994), 'International Maritime Boundaries: Political, Strategic, and Historical Considerations', *University of Miami Inter-American Law Review*, Vol. 26, pp. 243–295.

Parodi Nebreda, Daniel (2014), 'Extensión de la Frontera Marítima entre Perú y Chile: La Equidad Como Concepto Decisorio', *Revista de Derecho Universidad Católica del Norte*, Vol. 21 (2), pp. 495–510.

Pastene, Luis A. and Daniel Quiroz (2010), 'Outline of the History of Whaling in Chile', in Center for Folk Culture Studies, *Human Culture from the Perspective of Traditional Maritime Communities*, International Symposium Report No. 1, Kanagawa Shimbun Press, Kanagawa, pp. 73–98.

Phleger, Herman (1955), 'Some Recent Developments Affecting the Regime of the High Seas', *Department of State Bulletin* (January–June), Vol. 32, pp. 934–940.

Pineo, Ronn F. (2007), *United States and the Americas: Ecuador and the United States: Useful Strangers*, Athens, Georgia: University of Georgia Press.

Prescott, Victor and Clive Schoffield (2005), *The Maritime Boundaries of the World*, (second edition), Leiden: Martinus Nijhoff.

Quiroz, Daniel (2014), *Cazadores Modernos de Ballenas en las Costas de Chile (1905–1983)*, Santiago: Dirección de Bibliotecas, Archivos y Museos, Centro de Documentacion de Bienes Patrimoniales, p. 20.

Scheiber, Harry N. (2011), 'Taking Legal Realism Offshore- The Contributions of Joseph Walter Bingham to American Jurisprudence and to the Reform of Modern Ocean Law', in Robert W. Gordon and Morton J. Horwitz (eds.), *Law, Society, and History: Themes in the Legal Sociology and Legal History*, Cambridge: Cambridge University Press, pp. 337–363.

Selak, Charles B. Jr. (1950), 'Recent Developments in High Seas Fisheries Jurisdiction under the Presidential Proclamation of 1945', *American Journal of International Law*, Vol. 44 (4), pp. 670–681.

Sepúlveda, Jorge (1997), 'La Epopeya de la Industria Ballenera Chilena', *Revista de Marina* (Chile), Vol. 114 (November-December), pp. 1–18.

Shapiro, Sidney (1965), *The Fisheries of Chile*, United States Department of the Interior, Circular No. 234, Washington, DC.

Sorensen, Max (1958), 'Law of the Sea', *International Conciliation (Pamphlet 520)*, pp. 195–256.

Thiel, Martin et al. (2007), 'The Humboldt Current System of Northern and Central Chile', *Oceanography and Marine Biology, an Annual Review*, Vol. 45, pp. 195–344.

United Nations (2000), *Handbook on the Delimitation of Maritime Boundaries*, United Nations: Office of Legal Affairs.

Universidad Andrés Bello, Centro de Investigación Marina Quintay – CIMARQ (2017), http://ballenerosdequintay.unab.cl/cimarq/.

US Department of State (1955), 'Santiago Negotiations on Fishery Conservation Problems among Chile, Ecuador, Peru and the United States,

Santiago, 14 September to 5 October 1955', *Department of State Bulletin*, pp. 1025–1030.

US Department of State (Mimeo) (1955), *Santiago Negotiations on Fishery Conservation Problems*.

US Department of State (1979), Limits in the Seas, No. 86, Maritime Boundary: Chile-Peru.

US Naval War College (1956), *International Law, Situations and Documents*, Vol. 51.

US Naval War College (1959/60), *International Law Studies*, Vol. 53.

Villiger, Mark E. (2009), *Commentary on the 1969 Vienna Convention on the Law of Treaties*, Leiden: Martinus Nijhoff.

Waldock, C.H.M. (1956), 'International Law and the New Maritime Claims', *International Relations*, Vol. 1 (5), pp. 163–194.

Weisburd, A. Mark (2016), *Failings of the International Court of Justice*, Oxford: Oxford University Press.

Weissberg, Guenter (1967), 'Fisheries, Foreign Assistance, Custom and Conventions', *International and Comparative Law Quarterly*, Vol. 16 (3), pp. 704–724.

Widdows, Kelvin (1976), 'On the Form and Distinctive Nature of International Agreements', *Australian Yearbook of International Law*, Vol. 7, pp. 114–127.

Wiegand, Jane Shuttleworth (1969), 'Seizures of United States Fishing Vessels—The Status of the Wet War', *San Diego Law Review*, Vol. 6, pp. 428–446.

Yasseen, Mustafa Kamil (1976), 'L'interprétation des Traités d'après la Convention de Vienne sur le Droit des Traits', *Collected Courses of the Hague Academy of International Law*, Vol. 151 (III), pp. 1–114.

Young, Oran R. (1982), 'The Political Economy of Fish: The Fishery Conservation and Management Act of 1976', *Ocean Development and International Law*, Vol. 10, pp. 199–273.

Young, Richard (1949), 'Further Claims to Areas beneath the High Seas', *American Journal of International Law*, Vol. 43 (4), pp. 790–792.

Young, Richard (1951), 'The Legal Status of Submarine Areas beneath the High Seas', *American Journal of International Law*, Vol. 45 (2), pp. 225–239.

Zacklin, Ralph (1974), 'Latin America and the Development of the Law of the Sea: An Oveview', in R. Zacklin (ed.), *The Changing Law of the Sea, Western Hemisphere Perspectives*, Leiden: Sijthoff, pp. 59–77.

Index

200 nm claim: defined 7–8, 22–3, 37; defence of 25, 49; disregarded 55–6; enforcement 58, 72, 83, 90; and extension of the boundary 55; and Humboldt Current 10; and international law 64, 71–2, 88; and international solidarity 56; and islands 12–13, 28–30; and lateral boundary 3, 20, 62–3; and law of the sea 11, 73, 76–8, 80; and nature of the boundary 54; and negotiations with Bolivia 21; and third states 65, 75, 80, 82, 84; and whale hunting 48, 59–60

Accession Protocol 20–1
acquiescence 80–1
Alvarez, Judge Alejandro 81–2
anchovies 61–2
Aramburu y Menchaca, Andrés A. 23
Arica 22
Arosemena, Carlos Julio 83

Bar Association of Lima 23
Baxter, Richard 70, 73
Beckett, Sir Eric 38
Bedjaoui, Judge Mohammed 44
Bennouna, Judge Mohamed 76
Bhandari, Judge Dalveer 3, 31, 43, 48, 77
Black Sea case 71
Bolivia 20–2

CEP countries: 7–12, 19; and Accession Protocol 20–1; enforcement of the claim 83;

extension of the claim 23, 25, 40; negotiations with the US 73
civil law 42
Complementary Convention 25, 32–4, 37–8, 43, 46, 49, 93
connected treaties 7, 17–18, 22, 87
context 15–18, 32, 40–3
contiguous zone 22, 65, 72–3, 82, 91
continental shelf: 8–9, 21, 64–7, 72n3, 82, 86; and fisheries convention 74–5, 78, 82
Convention on Measures of Surveillance and Control 26
Convention on the Continental Shelf 65, 74
Convention on the Granting of Permits 26
Convention on the System of Sanctions 26
Convention on the Territorial Sea 65, 73
customary rules 14, 16

Denmark 8, 81
Donoghue, Judge Joan E. 84

EEZ 11, 71, 72n3, 73, 76, 86
economic development 9–10
ecosystem 10
Ecuador 7, 11–12, 19, 21, 24, 27–36, 47, 49, 59, 67–8, 82–3, 89, 91
environment 8, 10
Evensen, Jens 70
evidence 19–20, 22, 31, 34, 37, 40–3, 47–52, 54–7, 62, 76, 81, 84–5

equidistance method 3, 66n1, 67
ex aequo et bono 5, 85
extractive capacity 61, 88

FAO statistics 58, 60–3, 85
First Law of the Sea Conference 10,
  65, 73, 82
Fisheries Jurisdiction cases 78–80
fishery zone 79, 82
fishing 8, 25–6, 35, 39, 46–8, 52,
  55–63, 66, 70–1, 73–5, 77, 79,
  83–5, 89, 92
fishmeal 62

Gaja, Judge Giorgio 3, 31, 43,
  48, 77
García-Sayán, Enrique 10
geographical parallel 8n1, 66–7
guano 62

high seas 8, 48, 73–4, 95
Hito No.1 5n1, 20n2, 39
Humboldt Current 10, 59

Iceland 78–9, 82
India 82
Indonesia 82
Indus 58–9
inter se 53, 77–8, 90
intention of the parties 16–17, 30, 41,
  47, 64, 90
Inter-American Council of Jurists 81
Inter-American Juridical Committee 81
Inter-American Resolutions 68
Iquique 59
islands 12–15, 19, 27–31, 34, 41, 78,
  85, 87–8

Jiménez de Aréchaga, Eduardo
  11, 79

Koroma, Judge Abdul G. 44

Lauterpacht, Sir Hersh 9, 38
legal inference 46, 53, 85, 87
Lighthouse Arrangements 19n2,
  39–40, 48
Lima Agreements: 16, 18–19, 25, 36,
  42–3, 89

maritime boundary 5,11, 19n2, 21–2,
  30–1, 35–7, 39–41, 45
maritime zones 12–15, 18–19, 22–8,
  30–1, 34–5, 43, 48–9, 56, 59–60,
  72n3, 73, 78, 83, 85, 88–9, 91, 93
methods of delimitation 66, 68
Mexico 65, 82

natural resources 73, 76, 91–2
Norway 8, 58, 81–2

Onassis whaling fleet 27, 58–9, 88
ordinary meaning 14–18, 31, 38,
  40–3
Organization of American States 65
Orrego Vicuña, ad hoc Judge
  Francisco 3, 31, 43, 48, 77
Owada, Judge Hisashi 3, 50,
  52–4, 84

Pedra Branca case 50–1
Permanent Commission of the South
  Pacific 11, 83
practice of the parties 3, 12, 19–21,
  27, 52–8, 84, 88
protests 8, 80–1, 94

Quintay 59

Ranjeva, Judge Raymond 44

Sebutinde, Judge Julia 3, 50
Second Law of the Sea
  Conference 23
Sepúlveda-Amor, Judge Bernardo 3,
  46, 50, 52
Skotnikov, Judge Leonid 51, 77
small vessels 35, 37, 46–7, 55, 57–8,
  60–1, 63, 89, 95
soft law 89
South Korea 82
Special Agreement 13, 34–8, 40–1,
  43, 45–8, 50, 52–3, 55, 57–8, 63,
  87–9
standard clause 18–19, 32, 42, 49, 89
Sweden 8, 81

Tacna 22
Talcahuano 59

territorial sea: 21, 53; breadth of 3, 22, 68–70, 78, 81–2, 90; and fisheries jurisdiction 24, 64, 70–4, 79; and International Law Commission 65–6, 68
Third Law of the Sea Conference 11, 79, 82
Tomka, Judge (President) Peter 3, 43, 48, 77–8
Truman Proclamation 9, 65

UNCLOS 72–3, 76, 86
Unilateral Proclamations 7, 51, 57, 62, 65, 78
United Kingdom 8, 74, 78–9, 81–2

United States: 8–10, 70, 81; intervention in Ecuador 83; negotiations with CEP countries 73; proposals at law of the sea conferences 73–6

Valparaíso 59
Vienna Convention on the Law of Treaties 16–18, 40–2, 49

Waldock, Sir Humphrey 8, 16–17, 43, 70, 79–80
whale hunting 8, 47–8, 55, 57–63, 85, 89

Xue, Judge Hanqin 3, 31, 43, 48, 77

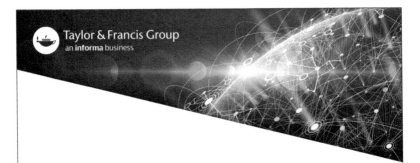

For Product Safety Concerns and Information please contact our EU representative GPSR@taylorandfrancis.com Taylor & Francis Verlag GmbH, Kaufingerstraße 24, 80331 München, Germany

Batch number: 08153772

Printed by Printforce, the Netherlands